I0625178

Tranquility

Unlock the Power of Tranquility: Discover Inner Peace, Overcome Stress and Anxiety, and Achieve Lasting Happiness with Proven Self-Help Strategies!

Lance P. Richards

Tranquility: Unlock the Power of Tranquility: Discover Inner Peace, Overcome Stress and Anxiety, and Achieve Lasting Happiness with Proven Self-Help Strategies!

Table of Contents

01: Understanding Tranquility: The Power of Inner Peace

Introduction

Tranquility is an essential aspect of our lives that we often overlook. It is the state of inner calmness and peace that enables us to face life's challenges with clarity, confidence, and resilience. However, in today's fast-paced world, finding tranquility can seem like an elusive dream. Stress, anxiety, and other mental health issues are on the rise, and many people struggle to find lasting happiness. This chapter aims to shed light on the power of tranquility and how you can unlock it to overcome stress and anxiety and achieve lasting happiness.

What is Tranquility?

Tranquility is a state of being that is characterized by a sense of inner calmness, peace, and harmony. It is a state where our thoughts and emotions are in balance, and we feel centered and grounded. Tranquility is not just about feeling relaxed or calm; it is a deeper state of being that encompasses all aspects of our lives. It is a state where we can find clarity, focus, and inner strength, even in the midst of chaos and uncertainty.

Tranquility is not a fixed state; it is a dynamic process that requires ongoing cultivation. It is not something that we can achieve once and for all; rather, it is a continuous journey that involves learning, growing, and evolving. The good news is that everyone can cultivate tranquility, regardless of their circumstances or background. It is a state that is available to all of us, and we can access it through self-help strategies and practices.

Why is Tranquility Important?

Tranquility is essential for our overall well-being and happiness. It has numerous benefits for our physical, mental, and emotional health, including:

Reducing Stress and Anxiety: Tranquility helps to calm our minds and reduce the impact of stress and anxiety on our bodies. It can lower our cortisol levels, reduce our blood pressure, and slow down our heart rate, all of which contribute to a more relaxed and peaceful state.

Enhancing Clarity and Focus: When we are in a state of

tranquility, our minds are clear, and we can focus better. We are less distracted by external stimuli and can concentrate on the task at hand more effectively.

Improving Emotional Well-being: Tranquility can help us to regulate our emotions better and improve our overall mood. We are less reactive to external triggers and can respond to situations with more compassion and understanding.

Boosting Resilience and Inner Strength: Tranquility helps to build our resilience and inner strength, enabling us to face life's challenges with greater confidence and ease.

Promoting Better Sleep: Tranquility can improve the quality of our sleep, enabling us to wake up feeling refreshed and energized.

How to Cultivate Tranquility

Cultivating tranquility requires a conscious effort and a willingness to explore different self-help strategies and practices. Here are some proven techniques that you can use to unlock the power of inner peace:

Mindfulness Meditation: Mindfulness meditation is a

powerful practice that involves focusing your attention on the present moment, without judgment. It can help to calm your mind, reduce stress and anxiety, and promote a sense of inner peace.

Yoga: Yoga is a physical and mental practice that can help to cultivate tranquility. It combines physical postures, breathing techniques, and meditation to promote relaxation, flexibility, and inner strength.

Deep Breathing: Deep breathing is a simple yet effective technique that can help to reduce stress and anxiety. It involves taking slow, deep breaths from the belly, which can calm the nervous system and promote a sense of relaxation.

Gratitude Practice: Gratitude is a powerful emotion that can help to cultivate tranquility. Practicing gratitude involves focusing on the things in your life that you are grateful for, which can shift your focus away from negative thoughts and emotions.

Nature Walks: Spending time in nature can help to promote tranquility and reduce stress and anxiety. Walking in nature can help to calm your mind and soothe your senses, allowing you to connect with your surroundings and feel a sense of inner peace.

Journaling: Journaling is a powerful tool that can help to promote self-reflection and self-awareness. Writing down your thoughts and emotions can help you to process them more effectively and reduce the impact of stress and anxiety on your mind and body.

Visualization: Visualization is a technique that involves imagining yourself in a peaceful and tranquil environment. This can help to promote relaxation and reduce stress and anxiety.

Mindful Breathing Exercises: Mindful breathing exercises are a series of breathing techniques that can help to promote relaxation and reduce stress and anxiety. These exercises involve paying attention to your breath and focusing your attention on the present moment.

Positive Affirmations: Positive affirmations are statements that you repeat to yourself to promote positive thoughts and emotions. This can help to shift your focus away from negative thoughts and promote a sense of inner peace and tranquility.

Self-Care: Self-care is a vital aspect of cultivating tranquility. Taking care of yourself physically, mentally, and emotionally can help to promote inner peace and reduce the impact of stress and anxiety on your life.

Conclusion

Tranquility is a powerful state that can transform your life. By cultivating inner peace and harmony, you can overcome stress and anxiety and achieve lasting happiness and fulfillment. The key is to explore different self-help strategies and practices and find what works best for you. By making tranquility a priority in your life, you can unlock the power of inner peace and transform your life in profound ways.

02: The Science of Stress and Anxiety: How They Impact Your Life

Stress and anxiety are common experiences that almost everyone faces at some point in their lives. They can be triggered by a variety of circumstances, including work, relationships, financial struggles, and health issues. In today's fast-paced society, stress and anxiety have become a chronic problem for many people, leading to a range of physical, emotional, and mental health issues.

The human body is designed to handle stress and anxiety in small doses, but prolonged exposure to stress can cause physical and mental exhaustion, resulting in a range of negative health effects. Chronic stress and anxiety can weaken the immune system, disrupt sleep patterns, raise blood pressure, and increase the risk of heart disease and other health problems.

To understand how stress and anxiety affect the body and mind, it is helpful to examine the science behind these conditions.

Stress is a natural response to perceived threats, whether

they are real or imagined. When the body senses danger, it activates the fight-or-flight response, a physiological reaction that prepares the body to either fight the threat or flee from it. This response is triggered by the release of stress hormones, including adrenaline and cortisol, which increase heart rate, respiration, and blood pressure.

The fight-or-flight response is essential for survival in dangerous situations, but it can also be triggered by non-threatening events, such as a difficult work meeting or a traffic jam. When stress is chronic, the body remains in a constant state of fight-or-flight, leading to a range of health problems.

Anxiety, on the other hand, is a feeling of unease or apprehension about a future event or situation. While stress is a response to a perceived threat, anxiety is a response to uncertainty or the unknown. Like stress, anxiety is a natural response that serves to protect us from harm, but chronic anxiety can lead to a range of negative effects.

Both stress and anxiety can affect the brain in a number of ways. Chronic stress can cause the hippocampus, the area of the brain responsible for memory and learning, to shrink in size, leading to memory problems and difficulty learning new things. Stress and anxiety can also cause the amygdala, the part of the brain responsible for emotions, to become overactive, leading to feelings of fear, anger, and sadness.

Chronic stress and anxiety can also affect the body in a number of ways. They can weaken the immune system, making it more difficult for the body to fight off infection and disease. They can also disrupt sleep patterns, leading to insomnia and daytime fatigue. Chronic stress and anxiety can also cause digestive problems, such as stomach ulcers and irritable bowel syndrome.

To manage stress and anxiety, it is important to identify the triggers that cause them and find ways to reduce their impact. Some proven self-help strategies include exercise, meditation, deep breathing, and cognitive-behavioral therapy.

Exercise is a natural stress reliever that can help reduce the symptoms of anxiety and depression. When you exercise, your body releases endorphins, which are natural mood-boosters that can help you feel better and more relaxed. Exercise can also help you sleep better, which can reduce the effects of stress and anxiety.

Meditation and deep breathing are also effective ways to manage stress and anxiety. When you meditate or practice deep breathing, you focus your mind on the present moment, which can help reduce feelings of worry and anxiety. Deep breathing can also help you slow down your heart rate and lower your blood pressure, which can help you feel more relaxed and calm.

Cognitive-behavioral therapy is a type of therapy that focuses on changing negative thought patterns and behaviors that contribute to stress and anxiety. Through this therapy, you learn to identify negative thoughts and replace them with more positive ones. You also learn coping skills and relaxation techniques that can help you manage stress and anxiety.

Another effective strategy for managing stress and anxiety is to develop a support network. Having supportive friends, family members, or a therapist to talk to can help you feel less isolated and more empowered to cope with difficult situations.

02: THE SCIENCE OF STRESS AND ANXIETY: HOW THEY IMPACT YOUR LIFE

In addition to self-help strategies, there are also a range of medical treatments available for managing stress and anxiety. These can include medications such as antidepressants and anti-anxiety drugs, as well as therapy options such as cognitive-behavioral therapy, exposure therapy, and dialectical behavior therapy.

It is important to note that not all treatment options work for everyone, and it may take some trial and error to find the right combination of strategies that work best for you. Additionally, it is important to seek professional help if your stress and anxiety symptoms are interfering with your daily life or causing significant distress.

While stress and anxiety are common experiences, it is possible to manage these conditions and achieve lasting happiness and inner peace. By understanding the science behind stress and anxiety and developing effective self-help strategies, you can learn to cope with life's challenges in a healthy and productive way. With the right tools and support, you can unlock the power of tranquility and achieve a more peaceful, fulfilling life.

03: The Benefits of Tranquility: What You Gain When You Find Inner Peace

The world we live in today is fast-paced, competitive, and demanding. With so much happening around us, it can be challenging to find inner peace and tranquility. However, when you do find inner peace, the benefits are immense. In this chapter, we will explore the many benefits of tranquility, including physical, mental, and emotional benefits.

Physical Benefits of Tranquility

When you are stressed, your body releases cortisol, the stress hormone. Cortisol can lead to a wide range of physical health problems, including high blood pressure, heart disease, diabetes, and obesity. However, when you find inner peace and tranquility, your body produces less cortisol, leading to improved physical health.

In addition, tranquility can also improve your sleep quality. When you are stressed, your mind is constantly racing, making it challenging to fall asleep or stay asleep. However, when you find inner peace, your mind is calm, and you can fall asleep more easily and stay asleep for longer periods.

Moreover, tranquility can also boost your immune system. When you are stressed, your immune system is weakened, making you more susceptible to illnesses and diseases. However, when you find inner peace, your immune system is strengthened, helping you to stay healthy and fight off illnesses.

Mental Benefits of Tranquility

The mental benefits of tranquility are equally as important as the physical benefits. When you find inner peace, you experience a sense of calm and clarity, which can improve your mental health.

Tranquility can reduce feelings of anxiety and depression. When you are stressed, anxious, or depressed, it can be challenging to see the positive side of things. However, when you find inner peace, you can view life more positively, leading to a reduction in feelings of anxiety and depression.

In addition, tranquility can also improve your cognitive function. When you are stressed, your mind is foggy, and it can be challenging to focus and make decisions. However, when you find inner peace, your mind is clear and focused, making it easier to concentrate and make decisions.

Emotional Benefits of Tranquility

The emotional benefits of tranquility are also essential. When you find inner peace, you experience a sense of emotional well-being, which can improve your overall quality of life.

Tranquility can improve your relationships with others. When you are stressed, anxious, or depressed, it can be challenging to connect with others. However, when you find inner peace, you can connect with others on a deeper level, leading to improved relationships and social support.

In addition, tranquility can also improve your self-esteem. When you are stressed, anxious, or depressed, it can be challenging to feel good about yourself. However, when you find inner peace, you feel more confident and self-assured, leading to improved self-esteem.

Tranquility can also lead to increased creativity. When your mind is calm and clear, you can tap into your creative side more easily, leading to improved creativity and problem-solving skills.

Conclusion

In conclusion, the benefits of tranquility are numerous and far-reaching. When you find inner peace, you can improve your physical health, mental health, and emotional well-being. You can reduce feelings of stress, anxiety, and depression, improve your sleep quality, boost your immune system, and improve your cognitive function. You can also improve your relationships with others, increase your self-esteem, and tap into your creative side more easily. So, if you haven't already, it's time to start your journey to inner peace and tranquility!

04: Developing a Tranquil Mindset: The Key to Achieving Lasting Happiness

As we navigate through life, we encounter countless challenges and obstacles that can cause stress, anxiety, and overwhelm. Whether it's the pressures of work, financial troubles, relationship issues, or health problems, the demands of modern life can take a toll on our mental and emotional well-being. In order to achieve lasting happiness and inner peace, it's essential to develop a tranquil mindset that can help us navigate these challenges with ease and grace.

The first step in developing a tranquil mindset is to understand the nature of the mind and how it works. The mind is a complex and multifaceted entity that is constantly in flux, responding to external stimuli and internal thoughts and emotions. When we allow our minds to be dominated by negative thoughts and emotions, such as fear, anger, and anxiety, we become trapped in a cycle of stress and negativity that can be difficult to break.

To develop a tranquil mindset, we need to learn how to observe our thoughts and emotions without becoming attached to them. This means cultivating a sense of mindfulness or awareness that allows us to step back from our thoughts and emotions and observe them as they arise, without getting caught up in them. By doing so, we can begin to gain control over our minds and develop a greater sense of inner peace and tranquility.

One of the most effective ways to cultivate mindfulness and develop a tranquil mindset is through the practice of meditation. Meditation involves sitting in a quiet and peaceful place and focusing your attention on your breath or a mantra. By doing so, you can train your mind to be more present and focused, reducing the impact of external distractions and internal chatter. Over time, this practice can help to calm your mind and reduce stress and anxiety.

In addition to meditation, there are many other practices and techniques that can help you develop a tranquil mindset. These include:

Yoga: Yoga is a physical and spiritual practice that involves a series of postures, breathing exercises, and meditation techniques. It can help to improve flexibility, strength, and balance, as well as reduce stress and anxiety.

Mindful Breathing: Mindful breathing involves focusing your attention on your breath as it moves in and out of your body. This practice can help to calm your mind and reduce stress and anxiety.

Gratitude: Cultivating a sense of gratitude can help to shift your focus from what you don't have to what you do have, increasing feelings of happiness and contentment.

Positive Affirmations: Positive affirmations are statements that you repeat to yourself to help reprogram your subconscious mind with positive thoughts and beliefs. They can help to counteract negative self-talk and increase feelings of self-worth and confidence.

Visualization: Visualization involves creating mental images of positive outcomes and experiences. This practice can help to reduce stress and anxiety by helping you to focus on positive possibilities rather than negative outcomes.

By incorporating these practices and techniques into your daily routine, you can begin to develop a tranquil mindset

04: DEVELOPING A TRANQUIL MINDSET: THE KEY TO ACHIEVING LASTING HAPPINESS

that will help you navigate life's challenges with greater ease and grace. You'll be better equipped to handle stress and anxiety, and you'll experience greater feelings of happiness and inner peace.

But developing a tranquil mindset isn't just about adopting specific practices and techniques. It's also about cultivating a broader set of attitudes and beliefs that support a tranquil way of life. These include:

Acceptance: Accepting that life is unpredictable and that challenges will arise is an important part of developing a tranquil mindset. When we resist or fight against the challenges that life presents, we create additional stress and anxiety. But when we accept these challenges as a natural part of life and focus on how we can grow and learn from them, we can cultivate a greater sense of peace and resilience.

Compassion: Developing a sense of compassion for ourselves and others is also essential to cultivating a tranquil mindset. When we approach ourselves and others with kindness, understanding, and empathy, we create a positive and supportive environment that can help to reduce stress and anxiety.

Mindful Communication: The way we communicate with ourselves and others can have a profound impact on our mental and emotional well-being. By practicing mindful communication, we can learn to express ourselves in a clear, respectful, and compassionate way, reducing the likelihood of misunderstandings and conflicts.

Gratitude: As mentioned earlier, cultivating a sense of gratitude can help to shift our focus from what we don't have to what we do have, increasing feelings of happiness and contentment. By taking the time to appreciate the good things in our lives, we can develop a more positive and optimistic outlook, reducing stress and anxiety.

Self-Care: Taking care of ourselves is an important part of developing a tranquil mindset. This means getting enough rest, eating well, exercising regularly, and taking time for activities that we enjoy. By prioritizing self-care, we can reduce stress and anxiety and improve our overall well-being.

Incorporating these attitudes and beliefs into your daily life can help you develop a more tranquil mindset, but it's important to remember that developing lasting change takes time and effort. It's not enough to simply adopt a few practices and expect to see immediate results. Instead, cultivating a tranquil mindset requires consistent effort and dedication over time.

As you work to develop a more tranquil mindset, it's important to be patient and compassionate with yourself. Remember that setbacks and challenges are a natural part of the process, and that it's okay to take things one step at a time. With consistent effort and dedication, you can develop the inner peace and tranquility that will help you achieve lasting happiness and well-being.

In conclusion, developing a tranquil mindset is essential to achieving lasting happiness and inner peace. By cultivating mindfulness, adopting positive practices and attitudes, and prioritizing self-care, you can reduce stress and anxiety and improve your overall well-being. Remember that developing lasting change takes time and effort, but with consistent dedication and compassion, you can achieve the tranquility and happiness you deserve.

05: Overcoming Negative Thoughts and Emotions: A Guide to Positive Thinking

Negative thoughts and emotions can be incredibly damaging to our mental health, well-being, and overall quality of life. They can lead to anxiety, depression, and a host of other issues, and can be particularly challenging to overcome.

Fortunately, there are many proven self-help strategies that can help us to shift our focus away from negative thoughts and emotions and cultivate a more positive and peaceful mindset. In this chapter, we will explore some of these strategies and provide practical advice on how to implement them in your daily life.

Identifying Negative Thoughts and Emotions

The first step in overcoming negative thoughts and emotions is to identify them. This can be challenging, as negative thoughts and emotions can be deeply ingrained and automatic. However, by paying attention to your internal dialogue and emotional responses, you can begin to recognize when you are experiencing negativity.

05: OVERCOMING NEGATIVE THOUGHTS AND EMO-
TIONS: A GUIDE TO POSITIVE THINKING

Common negative thoughts include:

– "I'm not good enough"

– "Nobody likes me"

– "I'm a failure"

– "I'll never succeed"

– "Everything always goes wrong for me"

Negative emotions may include:

– Anxiety

– Anger

– Sadness

– Fear

– Frustration

Once you have identified these negative thoughts and emotions, you can begin to take steps to address them.

05: OVERCOMING NEGATIVE THOUGHTS AND EMOTIONS: A GUIDE TO POSITIVE THINKING

Challenging Negative Thoughts

One of the most effective ways to overcome negative thoughts is to challenge them. Often, negative thoughts are based on inaccurate or distorted beliefs about ourselves or the world around us. By challenging these beliefs, we can begin to shift our perspective and cultivate a more positive mindset.

To challenge negative thoughts, ask yourself:

– Is this thought based on fact or opinion?

– Am I being too hard on myself?

– Is there any evidence to support this thought?

– How would I respond to a friend who expressed this thought?

By asking these questions, you can begin to break down the negative thought and find more accurate and positive ways of thinking.

Practicing Gratitude

05: OVERCOMING NEGATIVE THOUGHTS AND EMOTIONS: A GUIDE TO POSITIVE THINKING

Another powerful tool for overcoming negative thoughts and emotions is practicing gratitude. When we focus on the things we are thankful for, we cultivate a more positive mindset and reduce the power of negative thoughts and emotions.

To practice gratitude, try:

– Keeping a gratitude journal: Write down three things you are grateful for each day.

– Expressing gratitude to others: Thank people in your life for their support, kindness, and love.

– Focusing on the present moment: Take time to appreciate the beauty and wonder of the world around you.

By making gratitude a daily habit, you can begin to shift your focus away from negativity and towards positivity and peace.

Meditation and Mindfulness

Meditation and mindfulness are powerful tools for cultivating inner peace and overcoming negative thoughts and emotions. These practices help us to become more aware of our thoughts and emotions, and to develop a more compassionate and accepting mindset.

To practice meditation and mindfulness, try:

– Setting aside a few minutes each day to meditate or practice mindfulness.

– Focusing on your breath and letting go of distracting thoughts.

– Practicing self-compassion and accepting your thoughts and emotions without judgment.

Over time, these practices can help you to cultivate a more peaceful and positive mindset, and to overcome negative thoughts and emotions more easily.

Self-Care

Self-care is another important tool for overcoming negative thoughts and emotions. When we take care of ourselves, we feel more confident, empowered, and able to cope with stress and challenges.

05: OVERCOMING NEGATIVE THOUGHTS AND EMO-TIONS: A GUIDE TO POSITIVE THINKING

To practice self-care, try:

– Getting enough sleep each night.

– Eating a healthy and balanced diet.

– Engaging in regular exercise or physical activity.

– Taking time to do things you enjoy and that bring you pleasure.

By prioritizing self-care, you can improve your overall well-being and reduce the impact of negative thoughts and emotions.

Conclusion

Overcoming negative thoughts and emotions can be a challenging and ongoing process, but with the right self-help strategies, it is possible to cultivate a more positive and peaceful mindset. By identifying negative thoughts and emotions, challenging negative beliefs, practicing gratitude, meditation and mindfulness, and prioritizing self-care, you can overcome negativity and achieve lasting happiness and inner peace.

05: OVERCOMING NEGATIVE THOUGHTS AND EMOTIONS: A GUIDE TO POSITIVE THINKING

Remember, the key to overcoming negative thoughts and emotions is to be patient and persistent. Changing long-held beliefs and habits takes time, but with commitment and practice, you can create a more positive and fulfilling life.

It's important to also note that seeking professional help is always an option if you are struggling with negative thoughts and emotions that are interfering with your daily life. A therapist or counselor can provide additional support and guidance in overcoming these challenges and developing healthy coping strategies.

In the end, the power to overcome negativity lies within you. With the right mindset and self-help strategies, you can unlock the power of tranquility and achieve lasting happiness and inner peace.

06: Mindful Breathing: The Ultimate Self-Help Technique for Tranquility

As you sit there reading this book, take a moment to observe your breathing. Notice how your chest rises and falls with each inhale and exhale. Do you feel the coolness of the air as you breathe in, and the warmth as you breathe out? For most of us, breathing is something we take for granted. It happens automatically, without us even thinking about it. But what if I told you that by focusing on your breath, you could unlock the power of tranquility and achieve inner peace, overcome stress and anxiety, and achieve lasting happiness?

Mindful breathing is a powerful self-help technique that has been used for thousands of years to help people find inner calm and tranquility. It involves paying attention to your breath as you inhale and exhale, and focusing your mind on the present moment. When you practice mindful breathing, you become more aware of your thoughts and emotions, and you learn to accept them without judgment. This can help you to manage stress and anxiety, improve your mood, and enhance your overall well-being.

06: MINDFUL BREATHING: THE ULTIMATE SELF-HELP TECHNIQUE FOR TRANQUILITY

To get started with mindful breathing, find a quiet place where you won't be disturbed. Sit in a comfortable position with your back straight and your feet flat on the ground. You can close your eyes if it feels comfortable, or keep them open and focus on a spot in front of you. Take a few deep breaths, inhaling through your nose and exhaling through your mouth.

Now, begin to pay attention to your breath as you inhale and exhale. Notice the sensation of the air moving in and out of your nostrils. Follow the breath as it travels down into your lungs and fills your chest, and then as it leaves your body on the exhale. Try to focus all of your attention on your breath, and let go of any thoughts or distractions that come into your mind. If your mind begins to wander, gently bring it back to your breath.

As you continue to practice mindful breathing, you may begin to notice physical sensations in your body. You might feel tension or tightness in your muscles, or you might notice that your breathing becomes shallow or rapid when you're feeling stressed or anxious. By paying attention to these sensations, you can learn to identify when you're feeling stressed and take steps to manage your emotions.

One of the most powerful things about mindful breathing is that you can do it anywhere, at any time. Whether you're sitting at your desk at work, waiting in line at the grocery store, or lying in bed at night, you can always take a few moments to focus on your breath and find a sense of calm.

In addition to practicing mindful breathing on your own, there are also guided meditation apps and videos that can help you deepen your practice. These can be especially helpful if you're just getting started with mindfulness and want some guidance on how to focus your attention and stay present in the moment.

Mindful breathing is just one of the many self-help techniques that you can use to unlock the power of tranquility and find inner peace. By practicing this simple yet powerful technique on a regular basis, you can learn to manage stress and anxiety, improve your mood, and achieve lasting happiness. So take a deep breath, and let yourself be fully present in this moment. You deserve it.

07: Cultivating Mindfulness: How to Stay Present in the Moment

In today's fast-paced world, it's easy to get caught up in the hustle and bustle of life. We're constantly on the go, rushing from one task to the next, and rarely taking a moment to stop and breathe. This constant state of busyness can lead to stress, anxiety, and even burnout. That's where mindfulness comes in.

Mindfulness is the practice of staying present in the moment, without judgment. It's about being fully engaged in whatever you're doing, whether it's washing dishes, taking a walk, or having a conversation with a friend. When you're mindful, you're not lost in your thoughts, worries, or distractions. Instead, you're fully aware of your surroundings, your sensations, and your emotions.

Cultivating mindfulness takes practice, but it's worth the effort. Studies have shown that mindfulness can reduce stress and anxiety, improve mood, and even enhance physical health. In this chapter, we'll explore the benefits of mindfulness and provide practical strategies for incorporating mindfulness into your daily life.

07: CULTIVATING MINDFULNESS: HOW TO STAY PRESENT IN THE MOMENT

The Benefits of Mindfulness

Research has shown that mindfulness can have a wide range of benefits for both physical and mental health. Here are just a few of the ways that mindfulness can improve your wellbeing:

Reduce Stress and Anxiety: Mindfulness can help you manage stress and anxiety by teaching you to observe your thoughts and emotions without judgment. By staying present in the moment, you can avoid getting caught up in worries about the future or regrets about the past.

Improve Mood: Mindfulness can enhance positive emotions like joy, contentment, and gratitude. By staying present in the moment, you can savor the good things in life and cultivate a more positive outlook.

Enhance Focus and Productivity: Mindfulness can improve your ability to concentrate by reducing distractions and increasing awareness. By staying present in the moment, you can better focus on the task at hand.

Boost Physical Health: Mindfulness has been shown to

lower blood pressure, improve immune function, and reduce inflammation. By reducing stress and anxiety, mindfulness can also reduce the risk of heart disease, stroke, and
other chronic illnesses.

Increase Self-Awareness: Mindfulness can help you become
more aware of your thoughts, emotions, and behaviors. By
staying present in the moment, you can observe yourself
without judgment and make more conscious choices about
how you want to respond to the world around you.

Practical Strategies for Cultivating Mindfulness

Now that you know the benefits of mindfulness, let's explore some practical strategies for incorporating mindfulness into your daily life. Remember, mindfulness is a practice, so don't worry if it feels challenging at first. With time
and persistence, you can cultivate a more mindful way of
being.

Start with Breath Awareness: The breath is a powerful tool
for cultivating mindfulness. Start by taking a few deep
breaths, noticing the sensation of the air moving in and out
of your body. Then, try to maintain your focus on your

breath for a few minutes. Whenever your mind wanders, gently bring it back to your breath.

Practice Mindful Eating: Eating can be a great opportunity to practice mindfulness. Try to eat slowly and savor each bite, paying attention to the taste, texture, and aroma of your food. Avoid distractions like screens or conversation, and focus on the experience of eating.

Use a Body Scan: A body scan is a technique for bringing awareness to each part of your body, from your toes to your head. Start at your feet and work your way up, noticing any sensations you feel in each part of your body. This can help you become more aware of any tension or discomfort you're holding, and release it through deep breathing or gentle movement.

Take Mindful Breaks: Throughout the day, take a few mindful breaks to pause and reset. This could be as simple as taking a few deep breaths, stretching, or going for a quick walk outside. By taking these breaks, you can avoid getting caught up in the stress and busyness of daily life and stay present in the moment.

07: CULTIVATING MINDFULNESS: HOW TO STAY PRESENT IN THE MOMENT

Practice Gratitude: Gratitude is a powerful antidote to stress and anxiety. Take a few moments each day to reflect on what you're grateful for, whether it's a kind gesture from a friend, a beautiful sunset, or a warm cup of tea. By focusing on the good in your life, you can cultivate a more positive outlook and reduce stress and anxiety.

Engage in Mindful Movement: Mindful movement practices like yoga, tai chi, or qigong can be a great way to cultivate mindfulness and reduce stress. These practices involve slow, deliberate movements that are synchronized with the breath, helping you stay present in the moment and reduce distractions.

Practice Loving-Kindness Meditation: Loving-kindness meditation is a practice of cultivating feelings of kindness, compassion, and empathy towards yourself and others. Start by sitting in a comfortable position and focusing on your breath. Then, repeat a series of phrases like "May I be happy, may I be healthy, may I be safe," gradually extending the practice to include loved ones, acquaintances, and even people you may have difficulties with.

Set Mindful Intentions: At the beginning of each day, set an intention for how you want to approach the day ahead. This could be something as simple as "I intend to be present in my interactions with others" or "I intend to take breaks throughout the day to recharge." By setting these intentions, you can become more conscious of how you want to show up in the world and cultivate a more mindful way of being.

Incorporating mindfulness into your daily life takes time and practice, but the benefits are well worth the effort. By staying present in the moment, you can reduce stress and anxiety, improve mood, and enhance physical health. Whether you start with breath awareness, mindful eating, or loving-kindness meditation, there are many ways to cultivate mindfulness and unlock the power of tranquility.

08: The Power of Gratitude: Discovering Joy in the Simple Things

Introduction

In a world filled with chaos and stress, it can be easy to overlook the simple joys in life. We often take the little things for granted, and it's not until we lose them that we truly appreciate their value. But what if we could cultivate a mindset of gratitude and learn to find joy in the simple things every day? That's the power of gratitude, and it's a key component of achieving inner peace and lasting happiness.

What is Gratitude?

Gratitude is the quality of being thankful, showing appreciation, and recognizing the value of something. It's about acknowledging the good things in life, even when things seem tough or uncertain. Gratitude is not just a feeling, but a way of thinking and living.

Why is Gratitude Important?

Studies have shown that gratitude can have a positive impact on both physical and mental health. People who practice gratitude report lower levels of stress, anxiety, and depression. They also have stronger immune systems and better sleep patterns. Gratitude can also improve relationships, boost self-esteem, and increase overall happiness.

Gratitude can help us shift our focus from what we lack to what we have. It allows us to appreciate the small things in life and find joy in the present moment. When we practice gratitude, we are more likely to be kind, compassionate, and empathetic towards others.

How to Cultivate Gratitude

Gratitude is a mindset that can be cultivated through intentional practice. Here are some simple strategies to help you cultivate gratitude in your life:

Keep a Gratitude Journal

Take a few minutes each day to write down three things you are grateful for. It can be something as simple as a good cup of coffee or a phone call from a friend. Reflect on why you are grateful for each thing and savor the feeling of appreciation.

08: THE POWER OF GRATITUDE: DISCOVERING JOY IN THE SIMPLE THINGS

Practice Mindful Gratitude

Take a moment to pause and appreciate the little things in your life. Notice the beauty of nature, the warmth of the sun, or the sound of laughter. Practice being present in the moment and find joy in the simple things.

Express Gratitude to Others

Take the time to thank the people in your life who make a difference. Write a heartfelt note, send a text message, or simply say thank you. Expressing gratitude not only makes others feel appreciated but also reinforces your own sense of gratitude.

Shift Your Perspective

When faced with a challenging situation, try to reframe it in a more positive light. Look for the lessons learned or the opportunities for growth. Focus on what you can control and find gratitude in the present moment.

The Benefits of Gratitude

Practicing gratitude can have a profound impact on our

08: THE POWER OF GRATITUDE: DISCOVERING JOY IN THE SIMPLE THINGS

lives. Here are some of the benefits of cultivating a mindset of gratitude:

Improved Mental Health

Gratitude has been linked to lower levels of stress, anxiety, and depression. It can also improve resilience, helping us bounce back from adversity more quickly.

Better Physical Health

Grateful people have been shown to have stronger immune systems, better sleep patterns, and lower blood pressure. Practicing gratitude can improve overall physical health and wellbeing.

Stronger Relationships

Gratitude can improve relationships by fostering a sense of appreciation and empathy towards others. It can also increase feelings of social connectedness and reduce feelings of loneliness.

Increased Happiness

08: THE POWER OF GRATITUDE: DISCOVERING JOY IN THE SIMPLE THINGS

Gratitude has been shown to increase overall happiness and life satisfaction. When we focus on the good things in life, we are more likely to feel content and fulfilled.

Conclusion

Cultivating a mindset of gratitude can be a powerful tool for finding joy in the simple things in life. By taking the time to appreciate what we have, we can shift our focus from what we lack to what we have. Gratitude can improve our mental and physical health, strengthen our relationships, and increase overall happiness. By practicing gratitude regularly, we can train our brains to see the positive in every situation and find joy in the present moment.

It's important to remember that cultivating gratitude is not about ignoring or minimizing life's challenges. Rather, it's about acknowledging the difficulties we face while also recognizing the good things in our lives. When we practice gratitude, we build resilience and learn to approach challenges with a positive mindset.

Incorporating gratitude into our daily lives may feel daunting at first, but with practice, it can become a natural habit.

08: THE POWER OF GRATITUDE: DISCOVERING JOY IN THE SIMPLE THINGS

Whether it's through a gratitude journal, mindful appreciation, expressing gratitude to others, or shifting our perspective, there are many ways to cultivate gratitude in our lives.

As we cultivate a mindset of gratitude, we begin to see the world in a new light. We become more present, more joyful, and more connected to those around us. With the power of gratitude, we can unlock a deeper sense of inner peace and achieve lasting happiness.

09: The Art of Letting Go: Releasing Attachments and Finding Freedom

The concept of letting go is one that we hear about often in self-help circles, and for good reason. Holding onto negative emotions, past experiences, and even physical possessions can weigh us down and prevent us from living the fulfilling and joyful lives we desire. In this chapter, we will explore the art of letting go and how it can lead to greater tranquility, inner peace, and lasting happiness.

First, let's define what we mean by letting go. Simply put, it means releasing attachments to things that no longer serve us. These attachments can take many forms, such as:

– Emotional attachments to past traumas, grudges, or negative beliefs about ourselves

– Physical attachments to possessions that we no longer use or need

– Mental attachments to goals or expectations that no longer align with our true desires or values

09: THE ART OF LETTING GO: RELEASING ATTACHMENTS AND FINDING FREEDOM

– Spiritual attachments to beliefs or practices that no longer resonate with us

Letting go of these attachments is not always easy, and it can require a lot of inner work and self-reflection. However, the rewards of doing so are immense. When we release what no longer serves us, we make room for new opportunities, experiences, and growth.

One common attachment that many of us struggle with is the attachment to our own thoughts and beliefs. We may cling to certain ideas about ourselves or the world around us, even when those ideas are no longer serving us. For example, we may believe that we are not good enough, that we are unworthy of love, or that the world is a hostile and dangerous place. These beliefs can be deeply ingrained and may have been reinforced by past experiences or cultural conditioning.

To let go of these limiting beliefs, we must first become aware of them. This requires paying attention to our inner dialogue and noticing when negative or self-defeating thoughts arise. Once we have identified these beliefs, we can begin to challenge them by asking ourselves questions such as:

– Is this belief based on fact or opinion?

– Where did this belief come from, and is it still relevant to my current situation?

– What evidence do I have to support or refute this belief?

– How would my life be different if I let go of this belief?

By questioning our beliefs in this way, we can begin to loosen their hold on us and open ourselves up to new perspectives and possibilities.

Another common attachment that many of us struggle with is the attachment to material possessions. We may accumulate belongings over time, only to find that they clutter our physical space and drain our energy. Letting go of these possessions can be difficult, especially if we have sentimental attachments to them or if we worry that we might need them someday.

To release our attachment to material possessions, we can follow the principles of minimalism. This involves decluttering our living space and simplifying our possessions to only the essentials. We can ask ourselves questions such as:

– Do I use this item regularly, or is it just taking up space?

– Does this item bring me joy and enhance my life, or does it weigh me down?

– Am I holding onto this item out of fear or attachment?

By letting go of the possessions that no longer serve us, we create a more peaceful and harmonious living environment and free up our energy for more meaningful pursuits.

Letting go of attachments can also involve releasing relationships that no longer serve us. We may hold onto toxic or unfulfilling relationships out of habit or fear of being alone, but these relationships can drain our energy and prevent us from forming deeper, more meaningful connections.

To release toxic relationships, we can set healthy boundaries and communicate our needs and expectations clearly. We can also seek out new relationships that align with our values and bring us joy and fulfillment.

09: THE ART OF LETTING GO: RELEASING ATTACH-
MENTS AND FINDING FREEDOM

Finally, letting go can also involve releasing our attachment to outcomes and expectations. We may set goals for ourselves and become attached to a specific outcome, only to feel disappointed or defeated when things don't go as planned. We may also hold onto expectations of how our life should look or what we should achieve, based on societal or cultural norms.

To release our attachment to outcomes and expectations, we can practice mindfulness and acceptance. We can learn to be present in the moment and appreciate what we have, rather than focusing solely on what we want or don't have. We can also learn to embrace uncertainty and trust that the universe will guide us towards what is best for us.

In conclusion, the art of letting go is a powerful tool for achieving greater tranquility, inner peace, and lasting happiness. By releasing attachments to negative emotions, physical possessions, limiting beliefs, toxic relationships, and outcomes and expectations, we can create space for new opportunities and experiences that align with our true desires and values. While letting go can be challenging, it is a process that is well worth the effort. By embracing the art

09: THE ART OF LETTING GO: RELEASING ATTACH-MENTS AND FINDING FREEDOM

of letting go, we can unlock our full potential and live a more fulfilling and joyful life.

10: Transforming Fear and Anxiety: Overcoming the Obstacles to Inner Peace

Introduction:

Fear and anxiety are two of the most common and pervasive emotional states that we experience as human beings. They can be triggered by a range of stimuli, from perceived threats to uncertain situations to memories of traumatic events. Although fear and anxiety are natural responses that have evolved to help us survive, they can also become chronic and debilitating, robbing us of our inner peace and happiness.

In this chapter, we will explore the causes and effects of fear and anxiety and provide you with effective strategies for overcoming them. We will show you how to cultivate the inner resources that will enable you to respond to challenging situations with calmness, clarity, and confidence. By following these practices, you can transform fear and anxiety into opportunities for growth, healing, and transformation.

Section 1: Understanding Fear and Anxiety

10: TRANSFORMING FEAR AND ANXIETY: OVERCOM-ING THE OBSTACLES TO INNER PEACE

1.1 The Nature of Fear

Fear is a complex and multi-dimensional emotion that arises in response to a perceived threat or danger. It can be triggered by external stimuli, such as a loud noise, a sudden movement, or a threatening gesture, or by internal stimuli, such as a memory, a thought, or a feeling.

Fear is an adaptive response that has evolved to help us survive in the face of danger. It activates the sympathetic nervous system, triggering a series of physiological changes that prepare us for fight or flight. These changes include increased heart rate, rapid breathing, muscle tension, and heightened alertness.

Although fear can be a useful and necessary response in certain situations, it can also become chronic and excessive, leading to anxiety disorders such as panic disorder, social anxiety disorder, and generalized anxiety disorder.

1.2 The Nature of Anxiety

Anxiety is a state of chronic apprehension and worry that is characterized by excessive fear and uncertainty. It is a common response to stress and can be triggered by a range of situations, from social interactions to performance demands to uncertain future events.

Anxiety can be both a symptom and a cause of stress, as it can lead to physical symptoms such as headaches, muscle tension, and gastrointestinal problems, and can also increase the risk of developing other mental health conditions, such as depression and substance abuse disorders.

Like fear, anxiety is an adaptive response that has evolved to help us cope with the challenges of life. However, when it becomes chronic and excessive, it can interfere with our ability to function effectively and lead to a range of negative outcomes, including decreased quality of life, impaired social and occupational functioning, and increased risk of physical illness.

Section 2: The Causes of Fear and Anxiety

2.1 Biological Factors

Biological factors play a significant role in the development of fear and anxiety. Genetic factors can predispose individuals to certain anxiety disorders, such as panic disorder and phobias. Brain imaging studies have also shown that individuals with anxiety disorders have distinct patterns of brain activity that are associated with increased sensitivity to threat and decreased ability to regulate emotional responses.

2.2 Environmental Factors

Environmental factors such as traumatic events, stressful life events, and chronic stress can also contribute to the development of fear and anxiety. Traumatic events such as physical or sexual abuse, natural disasters, and accidents can lead to post-traumatic stress disorder (PTSD), a condition characterized by persistent and intrusive memories, nightmares, and avoidance behaviors.

Stressful life events such as divorce, job loss, and financial difficulties can also increase the risk of developing anxiety disorders. Chronic stress, such as that experienced by individuals in high-pressure jobs or caregiving roles, can lead to chronic anxiety and burnout.

2.3 Cognitive Factors

Cognitive factors such as negative thinking patterns, irrational beliefs, and cognitive biases can also contribute to the
development of fear and anxiety. Negative thinking patterns, such as catastrophizing, magnifying, and all-or-nothing thinking, can exacerbate feelings of fear and anxiety by
focusing on worst-case scenarios and undermining one's
sense of control.

Irrational beliefs, such as perfectionism, self-blame, and excessive worry about what others think, can also contribute
to the development of anxiety disorders. Cognitive biases,
such as selective attention, confirmation bias, and overgen-
eralization, can further reinforce negative thinking patterns
and exacerbate anxiety symptoms.

Section 3: Overcoming Fear and Anxiety

3.1 Mindfulness Meditation

Mindfulness meditation is a powerful practice for overcoming fear and anxiety. By focusing on the present moment
and observing one's thoughts and feelings without judgment, mindfulness can help individuals develop greater
awareness and control over their emotional responses.

Research has shown that regular mindfulness meditation can reduce symptoms of anxiety, depression, and stress, and increase feelings of well-being and inner peace. Mindfulness can also improve cognitive function, such as attention, memory, and decision-making, which can help individuals respond more effectively to challenging situations.

3.2 Cognitive Behavioral Therapy

Cognitive Behavioral Therapy (CBT) is a form of psychotherapy that has been shown to be highly effective in treating anxiety disorders. CBT works by helping individuals identify and challenge negative thinking patterns and beliefs that contribute to anxiety, and develop more adaptive coping strategies.

CBT typically involves a combination of cognitive restructuring, exposure therapy, and relaxation techniques. Cognitive restructuring involves identifying and challenging negative thinking patterns, such as catastrophizing and all-or-nothing thinking, and replacing them with more realistic and positive thoughts.

Exposure therapy involves gradually exposing individuals to

feared situations or stimuli in a safe and controlled environment, with the goal of reducing fear and anxiety over time.
Relaxation techniques, such as deep breathing and pro-
gressive muscle relaxation, can also help individuals reduce
physical symptoms of anxiety and promote feelings of
calmness and relaxation.

3.3 Lifestyle Changes

Making lifestyle changes can also be an effective way to
overcome fear and anxiety. Regular exercise, for example,
has been shown to be highly effective in reducing symptoms
of anxiety and depression, and promoting feelings of well-
being and inner peace.

Healthy eating habits, such as avoiding processed foods and
sugar, and consuming a balanced diet rich in whole foods
and nutrients, can also help individuals manage anxiety
symptoms. Getting adequate sleep, practicing good sleep
hygiene, and avoiding alcohol and caffeine can also promote
better sleep and reduce anxiety symptoms.

3.4 Social Support

Social support is also important for overcoming fear and anxiety. Having a strong support network of family, friends, and colleagues can provide individuals with emotional support, practical assistance, and a sense of belonging and connection.

Joining a support group or seeking professional help from a therapist or counselor can also be effective ways to overcome fear and anxiety. These resources can provide individuals with practical tools and strategies for managing anxiety symptoms, and offer a safe and supportive space to explore and process difficult emotions.

Conclusion:

Fear and anxiety are complex emotional states that can be triggered by a range of internal and external factors. Although fear and anxiety are natural responses that have evolved to help us survive, they can also become chronic and debilitating, robbing us of our inner peace and happiness.

By understanding the causes and effects of fear and anxiety, and implementing effective strategies for overcoming them,

individuals can transform fear and anxiety into opportunities for growth, healing, and transformation. By cultivating
the inner resources that enable us to respond to challenging
situations with calmness, clarity, and confidence, we can
unlock the power of tranquility and achieve lasting happiness and inner peace.

11: Creating a Tranquil Environment: How Your Surroundings Affect Your Mindset

Have you ever noticed how your surroundings affect your mood? How a cluttered room can make you feel anxious and overwhelmed, while a peaceful space can make you feel calm and relaxed? Our environment has a significant impact on our mindset, and creating a tranquil environment can help us achieve inner peace, overcome stress and anxiety, and achieve lasting happiness.

In this chapter, we will explore the importance of creating a tranquil environment and the strategies you can use to transform your surroundings into a peaceful oasis.

The Importance of a Tranquil Environment

Our environment can either support or hinder our mental health and wellbeing. Studies have shown that a cluttered and chaotic environment can contribute to stress, anxiety, and even depression. On the other hand, a peaceful and organized environment can have a calming effect on the mind, reduce stress, and improve our overall sense of wellbeing.

11: CREATING A TRANQUIL ENVIRONMENT: HOW YOUR SURROUNDINGS AFFECT YOUR MINDSET

Creating a tranquil environment is essential for anyone who wants to achieve inner peace and overcome stress and anxiety. When we surround ourselves with things that bring us joy and peace, we can create a sense of serenity that can help us cope with life's challenges.

Strategies for Creating a Tranquil Environment

Creating a tranquil environment doesn't have to be complicated or expensive. There are several simple strategies you can use to transform your surroundings into a peaceful oasis.

Declutter

One of the most important steps in creating a tranquil environment is to declutter your space. Clutter can be a significant source of stress and anxiety, so getting rid of things you no longer need or use can help create a more peaceful atmosphere.

Start by going through each room and sorting items into three piles: keep, donate, and discard. Be ruthless in your decluttering and let go of anything that no longer serves a purpose in your life.

Simplify

Once you've decluttered your space, simplify your surroundings by minimizing the number of items in each
room. A minimalist approach can help create a sense of
calm and serenity, so only keep items that are essential or
bring you joy.

Use Colors to Create a Mood

Colors can have a significant impact on our mood, so use
them to create a tranquil atmosphere. Soft, muted colors
like blues, greens, and grays can have a calming effect on
the mind, while bright colors can be energizing and stimulating.

Consider the mood you want to create in each room and
choose colors that support that goal. For example, blue is
often associated with tranquility and calmness, while green
can evoke feelings of relaxation and balance.

Add Plants

11: CREATING A TRANQUIL ENVIRONMENT: HOW YOUR SURROUNDINGS AFFECT YOUR MINDSET

Plants can help create a sense of tranquility by adding natural beauty to your surroundings. They also have several health benefits, including purifying the air and reducing stress levels.

Choose plants that are easy to care for and can thrive in your environment. Some good options include peace lilies, spider plants, and snake plants.

Let in Natural Light

Natural light can have a significant impact on our mood and energy levels, so make sure to let in as much natural light as possible. Open up blinds or curtains to let in sunlight and consider adding mirrors to reflect light and create the illusion of a larger space.

Eliminate Clutter with Storage Solutions

Now that you've decluttered and minimized, organize the remaining items with storage solutions. Add shelves, boxes, and baskets to keep items stored neatly and out of sight, eliminating clutter from your vision.

Incorporate Soothing Sounds

Sounds can help create a tranquil environment by masking unwanted noises and promoting relaxation. Consider adding soothing sounds like water fountains or white noise machines to create a peaceful atmosphere.

Set the Mood with Lighting

Lighting can help set the mood and create a peaceful atmosphere. Consider using soft, warm lighting to create a cozy and relaxing environment. Dimmer switches can also be used to adjust the lighting to the desired level, depending on the time of day and your mood.

Use Aromatherapy

Aromatherapy can help create a tranquil environment by promoting relaxation and reducing stress. Consider using essential oils, such as lavender or chamomile, to create a calming atmosphere. Diffusers can be used to disperse the scents throughout the room.

Add Comfortable Furniture

Comfortable furniture can help create a peaceful atmosphere by providing a cozy and inviting space to relax. Consider adding comfortable chairs, sofas, or pillows to create a comfortable and inviting space to unwind.

Remove Electronics

Electronics can be a significant source of stress and distraction. Consider removing electronics from your bedroom or creating a designated space for them to help create a peaceful environment. This can also help improve sleep quality, as the blue light emitted from screens can disrupt sleep patterns.

Personalize Your Space

Personalizing your space with items that bring you joy can help create a tranquil environment that reflects your personality and style. Consider adding artwork, photographs, or sentimental objects that evoke positive emotions and memories.

Conclusion

Creating a tranquil environment is essential for anyone who wants to achieve inner peace, overcome stress and anxiety, and achieve lasting happiness. By decluttering, simplifying, incorporating natural elements, and personalizing your space, you can create a peaceful oasis that promotes relaxation and supports your mental health and wellbeing. Take the time to transform your surroundings into a peaceful and serene environment, and enjoy the benefits of tranquility in your daily life.

12: Building Healthy Habits: Simple Steps to a More Tranquil Life

The pursuit of tranquility is a lifelong journey, and building healthy habits is an essential part of that journey. In this chapter, we will explore the simple steps you can take to create a more tranquil life by adopting healthy habits that will help you overcome stress and anxiety and achieve lasting happiness.

Before we dive into the specific habits that can help you achieve tranquility, let's take a moment to define what we mean by "healthy habits." A healthy habit is any behavior that promotes physical, mental, or emotional well-being. These habits can be as simple as taking a few deep breaths when you feel stressed or as complex as maintaining a regular exercise routine.

The key to building healthy habits is to start small and be consistent. Research has shown that it takes an average of 66 days to form a new habit, so it's important to be patient and persistent. Don't try to adopt too many habits at once, or you may become overwhelmed and give up. Instead, fo-

cus on one or two habits at a time and make them a part of
your daily routine.

Here are some simple steps you can take to build healthy
habits and create a more tranquil life:

Start with a morning routine: Your morning routine sets the
tone for the rest of your day. Start your day with a few
minutes of meditation or mindfulness practice to help you
clear your mind and focus on the present moment. You can
also incorporate gentle stretching or yoga to help you wake
up your body and get your blood flowing.

Practice gratitude: Gratitude is a powerful tool for promoting inner peace and happiness. Take a few minutes each day
to reflect on the things you are grateful for. You can write
them down in a journal or simply take a mental note.

Move your body: Regular exercise is essential for both physical and mental health. Find an activity that you enjoy,
whether it's running, cycling, swimming, or yoga, and make
it a part of your daily routine. Even a short walk around the
block can help you clear your mind and boost your mood.

12: BUILDING HEALTHY HABITS: SIMPLE STEPS TO A MORE TRANQUIL LIFE

Eat a healthy diet: Your diet plays a crucial role in your overall health and well-being. Aim to eat a balanced diet that includes plenty of fruits, vegetables, whole grains, and lean protein. Avoid processed foods, sugary drinks, and excessive alcohol consumption, as these can all contribute to stress and anxiety.

Get enough sleep: Adequate sleep is essential for both physical and mental health. Aim to get at least 7-8 hours of sleep each night and establish a regular sleep routine to help your body and mind prepare for rest.

Practice mindfulness: Mindfulness is the practice of paying attention to the present moment without judgment. Incorporate mindfulness into your daily routine by taking a few minutes each day to focus on your breath or simply observe your surroundings.

Connect with others: Human connection is essential for emotional well-being. Make time to connect with friends and family members, whether it's through a phone call, text message, or in-person visit. Joining a group or club that shares your interests can also help you feel more connected to others.

12: BUILDING HEALTHY HABITS: SIMPLE STEPS TO A MORE TRANQUIL LIFE

Take breaks: Taking breaks throughout the day can help you recharge and reduce stress. Schedule breaks into your daily routine, whether it's a quick walk around the block or a few minutes of deep breathing.

Practice self-care: Self-care is any activity that promotes physical, mental, or emotional well-being. Find activities that help you feel relaxed and rejuvenated, whether it's taking a warm bath, reading a book, or practicing a hobby you enjoy.

Stay organized: A cluttered environment can contribute to stress and anxiety. Take time to organize your living and working spaces, and establish systems to help you stay on top of your tasks and responsibilities.

Set goals: Setting and achieving goals can give you a sense of purpose and direction. Start by setting small, achievable goals and celebrate your progress along the way. You can also use a planner or journal to keep track of your goals and progress.

Practice self-reflection: Take time to reflect on your thoughts, feelings, and behaviors. This can help you identify patterns and make positive changes in your life. You can practice self-reflection through journaling, meditation, or simply taking a few minutes each day to check in with yourself.

Seek support: It's important to reach out for help when you need it. Whether you need professional support for a mental health issue or simply need to talk to a trusted friend, don't hesitate to ask for help when you need it.

Practice forgiveness: Forgiveness can be a powerful tool for letting go of negative emotions and promoting inner peace. Practice forgiveness towards yourself and others, and focus on moving forward rather than dwelling on the past.

Embrace imperfection: No one is perfect, and it's important to accept and embrace your flaws and imperfections. Focus on progress rather than perfection, and remember that mistakes and setbacks are a natural part of the learning process.

By adopting these simple habits and making them a part of your daily routine, you can create a more tranquil life and achieve lasting happiness. Remember, building healthy habits takes time and effort, but the rewards are well worth it. Be patient, stay consistent, and enjoy the journey towards inner peace and tranquility.

13: The Role of Nutrition and Exercise in Achieving Tranquility

Tranquility is a state of inner peace and calmness that can be elusive in today's fast-paced and stressful world. While there are many ways to achieve tranquility, the role of nutrition and exercise cannot be underestimated. In this chapter, we'll explore the connection between what we eat, how we move, and our ability to achieve lasting happiness.

Nutrition and Tranquility:

The food we eat plays a crucial role in our overall health and well-being. Our bodies require a balanced diet of protein, carbohydrates, fats, vitamins, and minerals to function properly. When we don't get the nutrients we need, our bodies can become depleted, leading to a host of health problems, including stress and anxiety.

One of the most important nutrients for achieving tranquility is magnesium. Magnesium is a mineral that helps to regulate our nervous system, promoting calmness and relaxation. Foods that are high in magnesium include leafy greens, nuts, seeds, and whole grains.

13: THE ROLE OF NUTRITION AND EXERCISE IN ACHIEVING TRANQUILITY

Another important nutrient for achieving tranquility is omega-3 fatty acids. Omega-3s are essential fats that help to reduce inflammation in the body, which can contribute to stress and anxiety. Foods that are high in omega-3s include fatty fish, such as salmon and tuna, as well as flaxseeds, chia seeds, and walnuts.

In addition to eating a balanced diet, it's important to pay attention to how we eat. Eating mindfully, or paying attention to the present moment and our bodily sensations while eating, can help us to feel more relaxed and centered. Mindful eating can also help us to make healthier food choices and prevent overeating.

Exercise and Tranquility:

Exercise is another important factor in achieving tranquility. When we exercise, our bodies release endorphins, which are natural mood boosters. Endorphins can help to reduce stress and anxiety, leading to a sense of calm and well-being.

In addition to releasing endorphins, exercise can also help us to focus our minds and increase our sense of self-efficacy. By setting and achieving fitness goals, we can build confidence in our abilities and feel a sense of accomplishment.

The type of exercise we do is also important. While any type of exercise can be beneficial, some forms of exercise are particularly effective at reducing stress and promoting tranquility. Yoga, for example, combines physical movement with deep breathing and meditation, helping to calm the mind and reduce stress.

Tai chi and qigong are also effective forms of exercise for promoting tranquility. These practices involve slow, gentle movements and deep breathing, which can help to quiet the mind and reduce stress.

Finding Tranquility Through Nutrition and Exercise:

To achieve lasting happiness and inner peace, it's important to prioritize both nutrition and exercise. By eating a balanced diet rich in magnesium and omega-3s, and exercising regularly with a focus on stress-reducing activities like yoga and tai chi, we can create a foundation of tranquility that will support us in all areas of our lives.

13: THE ROLE OF NUTRITION AND EXERCISE IN ACHIEVING TRANQUILITY

But achieving tranquility isn't just about what we eat and how we move. It's also about creating a balanced lifestyle that supports our mental, emotional, and spiritual well-being. This may involve cultivating healthy relationships, engaging in fulfilling work or hobbies, and finding time for relaxation and self-care.

Ultimately, achieving tranquility is a journey, not a destination. It requires a commitment to our own well-being and a willingness to make changes in our lives to support that well-being. By prioritizing nutrition and exercise, and cultivating a balanced lifestyle that supports our overall health and happiness, we can unlock the power of tranquility and achieve lasting peace and calmness in our lives.

14: Sleep and Tranquility: How a Good Night's Sleep Can Change Your Life

We all know how it feels to wake up after a good night's sleep. We feel refreshed, energized, and ready to take on the day. On the other hand, when we don't get enough sleep, we can feel tired, irritable, and have trouble concentrating. In fact, lack of sleep is one of the biggest culprits of stress and anxiety, and can have a profound impact on our physical and mental health.

In this chapter, we'll explore the importance of sleep for tranquility, how it impacts our well-being, and some self-help strategies to ensure you get the best possible sleep.

The Importance of Sleep for Tranquility

Sleep is a crucial component of our physical and mental health. It's during sleep that our body repairs and rejuvenates itself, and our brain processes the events of the day. A lack of sleep can have negative effects on our mood, cognitive function, and overall health.

Sleep is also important for managing stress and anxiety.

14: SLEEP AND TRANQUILITY: HOW A GOOD NIGHT'S SLEEP CAN CHANGE YOUR LIFE

When we're well-rested, we're better equipped to handle the challenges of daily life. Lack of sleep, on the other hand, can increase our stress levels, making it harder to cope with difficult situations.

The impact of sleep on our mental health is particularly significant. Studies have shown that people who don't get enough sleep are more likely to experience symptoms of anxiety and depression. Sleep deprivation can also exacerbate existing mental health conditions.

Finally, sleep is essential for achieving lasting happiness. When we're well-rested, we're more likely to feel positive emotions and be able to enjoy the good things in life. On the other hand, a lack of sleep can make us feel more negative and pessimistic.

The Effects of Sleep Deprivation

When we don't get enough sleep, we experience a range of negative effects on our physical and mental health. Here are some of the most common symptoms of sleep deprivation:

– Fatigue

– Irritability

– Mood swings

– Difficulty concentrating

– Memory problems

– Decreased cognitive function

– Increased stress and anxiety

– Depression

– Decreased immune function

– Weight gain

– Increased risk of chronic health conditions

As you can see, the effects of sleep deprivation are far-reaching and can have a profound impact on our well-being.

Self-Help Strategies for Better Sleep

Fortunately, there are many things we can do to improve the quality of our sleep. Here are some self-help strategies to help you get a good night's rest:

Stick to a sleep schedule - Go to bed and wake up at the same time every day, even on weekends.

Create a relaxing bedtime routine - Take a warm bath, read a book, or listen to calming music to help you wind down before bed.

Create a sleep-conducive environment - Make sure your bedroom is cool, dark, and quiet. Invest in a comfortable mattress and pillows.

Limit screen time before bed - The blue light from electronic devices can disrupt sleep. Avoid using electronic devices for at least an hour before bedtime.

Avoid caffeine, alcohol, and nicotine - These substances can interfere with sleep, so it's best to avoid them before bed.

Exercise regularly - Regular exercise can improve sleep quality, but avoid vigorous exercise too close to bedtime.

Practice relaxation techniques - Yoga, meditation, and deep breathing can all help you relax and prepare for sleep.

14: SLEEP AND TRANQUILITY: HOW A GOOD NIGHT'S SLEEP CAN CHANGE YOUR LIFE

Manage stress - Stress and anxiety can interfere with sleep. Practice stress management techniques such as mindfulness and cognitive-behavioral therapy.

Seek professional help - If you're struggling with sleep, don't hesitate to seek professional help. Your doctor or a sleep specialist can help you identify and address any underlying sleep disorders, such as insomnia or sleep apnea.

In addition to these self-help strategies, there are also some lifestyle changes you can make to promote better sleep:

Maintain a healthy diet - A balanced diet can promote better sleep by regulating hormones and promoting relaxation.

Limit alcohol and caffeine - As mentioned earlier, these substances can interfere with sleep, so it's best to avoid them or limit their consumption.

Reduce stress - Engage in activities that reduce stress such as spending time with loved ones, taking a relaxing bath, or listening to calming music.

Get regular exercise - Exercise can promote better sleep by reducing stress and anxiety.

14: SLEEP AND TRANQUILITY: HOW A GOOD NIGHT'S SLEEP CAN CHANGE YOUR LIFE

Create a peaceful sleep environment - Make your bedroom a calm and relaxing space by minimizing clutter and distractions.

Practice good sleep hygiene - This includes going to bed and waking up at the same time every day, avoiding naps, and avoiding stimulating activities before bed.

It's important to remember that getting a good night's sleep is a journey, not a destination. You may not see immediate results from these self-help strategies, but with consistency and patience, you can improve the quality of your sleep and achieve a greater sense of tranquility.

In conclusion, sleep is a crucial component of tranquility and well-being. Lack of sleep can have far-reaching negative effects on our physical and mental health, while getting enough sleep can help us manage stress and anxiety, and achieve lasting happiness. By adopting healthy sleep habits and lifestyle changes, you can improve the quality of your sleep and unlock the power of tranquility.

15: The Importance of Self-Care: Prioritizing Your Mental Health and Well-Being

In today's fast-paced and highly demanding world, it's easy to lose sight of the importance of self-care. We get so caught up in the daily grind of work, school, and family obligations that we often neglect our own needs. We put others first and forget that our mental health and well-being are just as important as any other aspect of our lives.

But the truth is, self-care is essential for a healthy and fulfilling life. It's not just about pampering yourself with spa days and shopping sprees (although those things are certainly nice). It's about taking care of your mind, body, and spirit in a way that promotes inner peace, reduces stress and anxiety, and helps you achieve lasting happiness.

In this chapter, we'll explore the importance of self-care and offer some proven strategies for prioritizing your mental health and well-being.

Understanding Self-Care

Self-care can be defined as any activity that we do deliberately in order to take care of our mental, emotional, and physical health. It's a way of nurturing ourselves, just as we would nurture a garden or a pet. It's about taking respons- ibility for our own well-being and making choices that pro- mote a healthy and balanced life.

Self-care looks different for everyone. For some, it might mean taking a long bath or reading a book. For others, it might mean practicing yoga or going for a run. It could also involve spending time with loved ones, journaling, or get- ting enough sleep. The important thing is that you find activities that work for you and prioritize them in your life.

Why Self-Care Is Important

Self-care is essential for our mental, emotional, and phys- ical health. When we neglect our own needs, we can quickly become overwhelmed, stressed, and anxious. We might also experience physical symptoms such as headaches, fatigue, and insomnia.

By taking care of ourselves, we can reduce stress and anxi- ety, increase our overall happiness and well-being, and im- prove our relationships with others. We can also boost our immune system and reduce our risk of developing chronic illnesses.

But perhaps the most important reason to prioritize self-care is that it allows us to live our best lives. When we take care of ourselves, we have the energy and motivation to pursue our passions, spend time with loved ones, and achieve our goals. We're better equipped to handle the ups and downs of life, and we're more resilient in the face of adversity.

Prioritizing Self-Care

Now that we understand the importance of self-care, let's explore some strategies for prioritizing it in our lives.

Make it a daily habit: Self-care shouldn't be something we only do when we have spare time. It should be a regular part of our daily routine. Set aside time each day for activities that promote your mental, emotional, and physical health. It doesn't have to be a lot of time – even 15 minutes can make a difference.

Identify your needs: Everyone's self-care needs are different. Take some time to reflect on what activities make you feel calm, relaxed, and happy. Do you need alone time to recharge? Do you enjoy spending time in nature? Once you've identified your needs, prioritize them in your life.

Set boundaries: One of the biggest obstacles to self-care is a lack of boundaries. We often feel guilty for saying no to others or setting aside time for ourselves. But setting boundaries is essential for our well-being. Learn to say no when you need to, and don't feel guilty about taking time for yourself.

Get support: Self-care is much easier when we have support from others. Talk to friends and family about your self-care goals, and ask for their help when you need it. You might also consider joining a support group or seeing a therapist.

Practice mindfulness: Mindfulness is a powerful tool for reducing stress and promoting inner peace. Try incorporating mindfulness into your daily routine by practicing meditation, deep breathing exercises, or simply taking a few moments each day to focus on the present moment.

Prioritize sleep: Sleep is essential for our mental and physical health. Make sure you're getting enough sleep each night – aim for seven to nine hours – and create a relaxing bedtime routine to help you unwind and prepare for sleep.

Move your body: Regular exercise is essential for our physical and mental health. Find a form of exercise that you enjoy – whether it's jogging, yoga, or dancing – and make it a regular part of your routine.

Eat well: A healthy diet is essential for our overall health and well-being. Focus on eating a balanced diet that includes plenty of fruits, vegetables, whole grains, and lean protein. Avoid processed foods and sugary drinks, which can cause mood swings and energy crashes.

Unplug: In today's digital age, it's easy to become overwhelmed by constant notifications and information overload. Take regular breaks from technology to give your mind a rest and recharge your batteries.

Practice self-compassion: Finally, remember to be kind and compassionate to yourself. It's easy to beat ourselves up when we fall short of our goals or make mistakes. But self-compassion is essential for our mental health and well-being. Treat yourself with the same kindness and understand-

15: THE IMPORTANCE OF SELF-CARE: PRIORITIZING YOUR MENTAL HEALTH AND WELL-BEING

ing that you would offer a friend.

In conclusion, self-care is essential for our mental, emotional, and physical health. By prioritizing self-care in our daily lives, we can reduce stress and anxiety, increase our overall happiness and well-being, and achieve lasting happiness. So take some time today to identify your self-care needs and prioritize them in your life – you deserve it!

16: Mindful Relationships: How to Cultivate Loving and Supportive Connections

In this chapter, we will explore the topic of mindful relationships and how they can help you cultivate loving and supportive connections in your life. We will discuss the importance of mindfulness in relationships, how to develop mindfulness in yourself, and how to use mindfulness to improve your relationships with others.

What is Mindfulness?

Before we dive into the topic of mindful relationships, let's first define what mindfulness is. Mindfulness is the practice of paying attention to the present moment without judgment. It involves being aware of your thoughts, feelings, and sensations in the present moment, and accepting them without trying to change them.

The practice of mindfulness can help you reduce stress, anxiety, and depression, as well as increase your overall well-being. It can also help you improve your relationships with others by allowing you to be more present and attentive to their needs.

88

16: MINDFUL RELATIONSHIPS: HOW TO CULTIVATE LOVING AND SUPPORTIVE CONNECTIONS

Why Mindfulness is Important in Relationships?

Mindfulness is important in relationships because it helps you to be more present and attentive to your partner's needs. It can also help you to communicate more effectively, reduce conflict, and build a deeper connection with your partner.

When you are mindful, you are able to pay attention to your partner in a non-judgmental way. You can listen to what they are saying, understand their perspective, and respond in a compassionate and supportive way.

On the other hand, when you are not mindful, you may be more reactive to your partner's words and actions. You may jump to conclusions, make assumptions, or become defensive. This can lead to misunderstandings, hurt feelings, and conflict in your relationship.

How to Develop Mindfulness in Yourself?

If you want to cultivate mindfulness in your relationships, you first need to develop mindfulness in yourself. Here are some tips for developing mindfulness:

16: MINDFUL RELATIONSHIPS: HOW TO CULTIVATE LOVING AND SUPPORTIVE CONNECTIONS

Practice mindfulness meditation: One of the most effective ways to develop mindfulness is through meditation. You can start by setting aside a few minutes each day to sit quietly and focus on your breath. When your mind wanders, simply bring your attention back to your breath.

Engage in mindful activities: You can also develop mindfulness by engaging in activities that require your full attention, such as yoga, tai chi, or hiking. These activities can help you to be more present and attentive to your surroundings.

Practice mindful breathing: Whenever you feel stressed or overwhelmed, take a few deep breaths and focus on your breath. This can help to calm your mind and reduce anxiety.

Practice self-compassion: Be kind and compassionate to yourself, even when you make mistakes or face challenges. Treat yourself with the same kindness and compassion you would show to a good friend.

How to Use Mindfulness to Improve Your Relationships?

Once you have developed mindfulness in yourself, you can

use it to improve your relationships with others. Here are some tips for using mindfulness to improve your relationships:

Practice active listening: When you are having a conversation with your partner, practice active listening by giving them your full attention. This means putting aside distractions and focusing on what they are saying.

Practice empathy: Try to understand your partner's perspective by putting yourself in their shoes. This can help you to be more compassionate and supportive in your interactions.

Respond, don't react: When your partner says something that triggers a negative emotion in you, try to respond rather than react. Take a deep breath and consider your response before speaking.

Practice gratitude: Take time each day to reflect on the things you appreciate about your partner. This can help you to focus on the positive aspects of your relationship and increase feelings of love and connection.

Conclusion

In conclusion, developing mindfulness in yourself and using it to improve your relationships can have a profound impact on your overall well-being and happiness. By practicing active listening, empathy, and gratitude, and responding rather than reacting to your partner's words and actions, you can cultivate a deeper and more loving connection with them.

Remember, mindfulness is not a quick fix solution for relationship issues, but it is a powerful tool for cultivating a healthy and supportive relationship over time. It requires consistent practice and effort to develop mindfulness in yourself and apply it to your relationships.

However, the benefits of mindful relationships are well worth the effort. Mindful relationships can help you to communicate more effectively, reduce conflict, and build a deeper connection with your partner. They can also help you to cultivate inner peace and happiness, which can positively impact all areas of your life.

So, if you want to improve your relationships and cultivate

more inner peace and happiness in your life, start by developing mindfulness in yourself. With consistent practice and
effort, you can unlock the power of mindfulness and transform your relationships and your life.

17: The Power of Forgiveness: Letting Go of Resentment and Anger

Introduction

Forgiveness is one of the most powerful tools that we have for finding inner peace and achieving lasting happiness. When we hold onto anger, resentment, and other negative emotions, we create a toxic environment within ourselves that can lead to stress, anxiety, and even physical illness. But when we learn to forgive, we open ourselves up to a world of possibilities and free ourselves from the burden of past hurts.

In this chapter, we will explore the power of forgiveness and how it can help us overcome stress and anxiety and achieve lasting happiness. We will look at what forgiveness is, why it is important, and how we can develop forgiveness as a habit in our lives.

What is Forgiveness?

Forgiveness is the act of letting go of anger, resentment, and other negative emotions towards someone who has wronged us. It is a conscious decision to release the person from the emotional debt they owe us and move on from the situation.

Forgiveness does not mean that we condone or forget what the person did to us. Instead, it means that we are choosing to release the negative emotions and not let them control our lives. Forgiveness is not easy, and it often requires a lot of inner work, but it is essential for our mental and emotional well-being.

Why is Forgiveness Important?

Forgiveness is essential for our mental and emotional well-being. When we hold onto anger, resentment, and other negative emotions, we create a toxic environment within ourselves that can lead to stress, anxiety, and even physical illness. Holding onto negative emotions can also impact our relationships with others and prevent us from experiencing true happiness.

Forgiveness can help us to break free from the cycle of negative emotions and find inner peace. It can also improve our relationships with others by allowing us to let go of past hurts and move forward with a clean slate. When we forgive, we are not only helping ourselves, but we are also helping the person who wronged us by releasing them from the emotional debt they owe us.

How Can We Develop Forgiveness as a Habit?

Developing forgiveness as a habit takes time and effort, but it is worth it. Here are some strategies that can help us develop forgiveness as a habit in our lives:

Practice Empathy

One of the best ways to develop forgiveness as a habit is to practice empathy. When we put ourselves in the other person's shoes and try to understand their perspective, we can begin to see things from their point of view. This can help us to let go of anger and resentment and develop compassion towards the person who wronged us.

Focus on the Present

When we hold onto past hurts, we prevent ourselves from living in the present moment. Instead of dwelling on the past, we can choose to focus on the present and the positive things in our lives. This can help us to let go of negative emotions and move forward with our lives.

Learn from the Experience

Every experience, no matter how negative, can teach us something. When we approach the situation with an open mind and a willingness to learn, we can gain valuable insights that can help us to grow and develop as individuals. This can help us to let go of negative emotions and move on from the situation.

Practice Self-Compassion

Forgiving ourselves is just as important as forgiving others. When we make mistakes, it is easy to beat ourselves up and hold onto negative emotions. But when we practice self-compassion, we can learn to forgive ourselves and move forward with our lives. This can help us to let go of negative emotions and find inner peace.

Seek Support

Forgiveness is not always easy, and sometimes we need help from others to develop forgiveness as a habit. Seeking support from a trusted friend, family member, or therapist can provide us with the guidance and encouragement we need to let go of negative emotions and move forward with our lives.

Practice Mindfulness

Mindfulness is the practice of being present in the moment and accepting our thoughts and emotions without judgment. When we practice mindfulness, we can observe our thoughts and emotions without getting caught up in them. This can help us to let go of negative emotions and find inner peace.

Practice Gratitude

Gratitude is the practice of focusing on the positive things in our lives and expressing appreciation for them. When we practice gratitude, we shift our focus from the negative to the positive, which can help us to let go of negative emotions and find inner peace.

Practice Forgiveness Daily

Forgiveness is not a one-time event; it is a daily practice. Every day, we encounter situations that can trigger negative emotions, and it is important to practice forgiveness daily to develop it as a habit. We can do this by setting aside time each day to reflect on our emotions and practice forgiveness.

Conclusion

Forgiveness is a powerful tool that can help us find inner peace, overcome stress and anxiety, and achieve lasting happiness. It is essential for our mental and emotional well-being, and developing forgiveness as a habit can have a profound impact on our lives.

By practicing empathy, focusing on the present, learning from the experience, practicing self-compassion, seeking support, practicing mindfulness, practicing gratitude, and practicing forgiveness daily, we can develop forgiveness as a habit in our lives and experience the many benefits that come with it.

Letting go of resentment and anger is not always easy, but it is worth it. When we choose to forgive, we are choosing to free ourselves from the burden of past hurts and open ourselves up to a world of possibilities. So let us practice

17: THE POWER OF FORGIVENESS: LETTING GO OF RE-SENTMENT AND ANGER

forgiveness daily and unlock the power of tranquility in our lives.

18: The Art of Listening: How to Build Stronger Relationships

Have you ever had a conversation with someone and felt like they weren't really listening to you? Or maybe you were the one who wasn't fully present in the moment, distracted by your own thoughts or concerns. It's a common experience, and one that can have a negative impact on our relationships with others. But the good news is that the art of listening is something that can be developed and improved upon, leading to deeper connections and stronger relationships.

In this chapter, we'll explore the importance of listening and how to become a better listener. We'll also look at some common barriers to effective listening and provide practical strategies for overcoming them.

The Power of Listening

Listening is one of the most important skills we can develop in our relationships with others. When we listen, we show that we care about the other person and their perspective. It also allows us to gain a better understanding of their thoughts and feelings, and can help to build trust and empathy.

Effective listening can also lead to more productive and successful conversations. By truly hearing and understanding what someone else is saying, we can work together to find solutions, make decisions, and collaborate on projects.

On the other hand, when we don't listen, we send the message that we don't value the other person's input or perspective. This can lead to misunderstandings, hurt feelings, and even conflict. It can also prevent us from learning and growing as individuals, as we miss out on opportunities to expand our own understanding and knowledge.

Barriers to Effective Listening

There are several common barriers to effective listening, including:

Distractions: We live in a world full of distractions, from our phones and social media to the noise and activity around us. When we're distracted, it's difficult to give our full attention to the person we're talking to.

Preconceived Ideas: We all have our own preconceived

ideas and biases that can prevent us from truly hearing and understanding someone else's perspective.

Emotional Reactions: When we're emotionally triggered, it can be hard to remain calm and present in a conversation. Our emotions can cloud our ability to listen objectively and empathetically.

Multitasking: Trying to do too many things at once, such as checking emails or doing other work while in a conversation, can prevent us from fully focusing on the person we're talking to.

Lack of Interest: If we're not interested in the topic or the person we're talking to, it can be difficult to stay engaged and focused.

Strategies for Effective Listening

Fortunately, there are several strategies we can use to overcome these barriers and become better listeners:

Be Present: Make a conscious effort to be fully present in the moment when you're in a conversation with someone. Put away distractions and focus your attention on the person in front of you.

Listen with an Open Mind: Try to approach each conversation with an open mind and a willingness to learn something new. Be aware of your own biases and try to set them aside to truly hear what the other person is saying.

Practice Empathy: Put yourself in the other person's shoes and try to understand their perspective. Acknowledge their feelings and show that you care about their experience.

Stay Calm: If you're emotionally triggered during a conversation, take a moment to breathe and calm yourself before continuing. This will help you stay objective and focused on the conversation.

Avoid Multitasking: When you're in a conversation with someone, give them your full attention. Avoid checking your phone or doing other tasks that might distract you from the conversation.

Show Interest: Even if you're not initially interested in the topic or the person you're talking to, try to find something to be curious about. Ask questions and show that you're interested in learning more about them and their experiences.

Paraphrase: One of the most effective ways to demonstrate that you're truly listening is to paraphrase what the other person has said. This shows that you're actively processing their words and trying to understand their meaning.

Ask for Clarification: If you're unsure about something the other person has said, don't be afraid to ask for clarification. This shows that you're engaged in the conversation and want to make sure you understand their perspective.

Practice Active Listening: Active listening involves fully engaging in the conversation and responding with both verbal and nonverbal cues. This includes making eye contact, nodding, and using affirming statements like "I see," or "That makes sense."

Be Patient: Effective listening requires patience, especially when dealing with complex or emotional topics. Allow the other person to fully express themselves before responding, and don't interrupt or rush the conversation.

Putting it into Practice

18: THE ART OF LISTENING: HOW TO BUILD STRONGER RELATIONSHIPS

Improving your listening skills takes practice, but the benefits are well worth the effort. Here are some tips for putting these strategies into practice:

Start Small: Begin by practicing your listening skills in low-stakes conversations, such as with friends or family members. As you become more comfortable, you can work your way up to more challenging conversations.

Reflect on Your Conversations: After a conversation, take a few moments to reflect on how well you listened. Were there any barriers that prevented you from fully engaging? Were there any strategies that worked particularly well?

Seek Feedback: Ask friends or family members for feedback on your listening skills. What do they think you could do better? What strategies did they find most effective when talking to you?

Practice Mindful Listening: Mindful listening involves being fully present and engaged in the conversation without judgment or distraction. Try practicing mindfulness exercises before engaging in a conversation to help you stay present and focused.

18: THE ART OF LISTENING: HOW TO BUILD STRONGER RELATIONSHIPS

Take a Listening Course: There are many courses and workshops available that focus specifically on improving listening skills. Consider taking one of these courses to learn more about effective listening strategies and practice them in a supportive environment.

In conclusion, the art of listening is a crucial component of building strong and meaningful relationships. By practicing effective listening strategies, we can deepen our connections with others, overcome conflicts and misunderstandings, and achieve greater understanding and empathy. So take the time to listen, be present, and engage fully in your conversations, and watch as your relationships grow stronger and more fulfilling.

19: Finding Tranquility in Nature: The Healing Power of the Outdoors

Introduction

In today's fast-paced and technology-driven world, we are constantly bombarded with information, deadlines, and stressors. It is no wonder that stress and anxiety have become a common part of our daily lives. While there are many ways to cope with stress and anxiety, one of the most effective and natural ways is to spend time in nature. In this chapter, we will explore the healing power of the outdoors and how we can find tranquility in nature.

The Healing Power of Nature

Nature has a profound healing power that can benefit our physical, emotional, and mental well-being. Research has shown that spending time in nature can reduce stress, anxiety, and depression, and improve mood and cognitive function. In fact, a study conducted by the University of Michigan found that just a 20-minute walk in nature can significantly reduce cortisol levels, which is the hormone associated with stress.

19: FINDING TRANQUILITY IN NATURE: THE HEALING POWER OF THE OUTDOORS

One reason why nature is so beneficial to our health is that it provides a sense of tranquility and calmness that can be difficult to find in our busy lives. When we are in nature, we are surrounded by beauty, stillness, and serenity, which can help us relax and recharge.

The Benefits of Being Outdoors

Being outdoors can offer a variety of benefits beyond reducing stress and anxiety. Some of the most significant benefits include:

Boosting Vitamin D levels: Sun exposure is an excellent source of Vitamin D, which is essential for strong bones, a healthy immune system, and overall well-being.

Increasing physical activity: Being outside encourages physical activity, which is crucial for maintaining a healthy weight, preventing chronic diseases, and improving overall physical health.

Improving sleep: Exposure to natural light during the day and darkness at night helps regulate the body's circadian rhythm, which can improve sleep quality.

19: FINDING TRANQUILITY IN NATURE: THE HEALING POWER OF THE OUTDOORS

Enhancing creativity and productivity: Being in nature can improve creativity, increase focus, and enhance productivity, making it an excellent place to work or study.

Finding Tranquility in Nature

Now that we understand the benefits of being outdoors, let's explore how we can find tranquility in nature.

Mindful Walking: One of the simplest and most effective ways to find tranquility in nature is by practicing mindful walking. Mindful walking involves paying attention to your breath and the sensations in your body as you walk. This can help you stay present in the moment and appreciate the beauty of nature around you.

Forest Bathing: Forest bathing, or Shinrin-yoku, is a Japanese practice that involves immersing oneself in nature to promote healing and relaxation. This involves walking in a forest, taking deep breaths, and connecting with the environment around you.

Yoga and Meditation: Practicing yoga and meditation in nature can help you find inner peace and tranquility. Find a quiet spot outdoors and practice your favorite yoga poses or meditation techniques while connecting with the natural environment.

Nature Photography: Engaging in nature photography can help you appreciate the beauty of nature and find tranquility in the process. Take your camera or smartphone with you on a nature walk and capture the beauty around you.

Conclusion

Finding tranquility in nature is a powerful way to reduce stress and anxiety and improve overall well-being. Whether you choose to practice mindful walking, forest bathing, yoga and meditation, or nature photography, spending time in nature can help you find inner peace and tranquility. So next time you feel overwhelmed, take a break and go outside. You might be surprised at how much better you feel.

20: Meditation for Tranquility: Different Techniques to Find Inner Peace

Meditation is one of the most powerful tools we have to achieve tranquility. It is a practice that has been used for centuries by people of all backgrounds, cultures, and religions. Meditation can help us to calm our minds, reduce stress and anxiety, and connect with our inner selves. In this chapter, we will explore the different techniques of meditation that can help you find inner peace and tranquility.

Mindfulness Meditation:

Mindfulness meditation is a type of meditation that involves being present and fully engaged in the present moment. It is about paying attention to your thoughts, feelings, and sensations without judgment. Mindfulness meditation can help you to stay focused, reduce anxiety and stress, and increase your overall well-being.

To practice mindfulness meditation, find a quiet and comfortable place to sit or lie down. Close your eyes and take a few deep breaths, focusing on the sensation of air moving in

and out of your body. Bring your attention to the present
moment, and notice any thoughts, feelings, or sensations
that arise.

Loving-Kindness Meditation:

Loving-kindness meditation is a practice that involves dir-
ecting positive thoughts and feelings towards yourself and
others. It is about cultivating feelings of love, kindness, and
compassion towards yourself and others. Loving-kindness
meditation can help you to reduce negative emotions, increase positive emotions, and improve your relationships
with others.

To practice loving-kindness meditation, find a quiet and
comfortable place to sit or lie down. Close your eyes and
take a few deep breaths, focusing on the sensation of air
moving in and out of your body. Visualize yourself and others, and repeat phrases such as "may I be happy, may I be
healthy, may I be safe, may I live with ease." You can also
direct these phrases towards others, such as your loved
ones, friends, and even strangers.

Transcendental Meditation:

20: MEDITATION FOR TRANQUILITY: DIFFERENT TECHNIQUES TO FIND INNER PEACE

Transcendental meditation is a type of meditation that involves the use of a mantra, or a word or phrase that is repeated silently. It is a simple and easy-to-learn technique that can help you to reduce stress and anxiety, improve your sleep, and increase your overall well-being.

To practice transcendental meditation, find a quiet and comfortable place to sit or lie down. Close your eyes and take a few deep breaths, focusing on the sensation of air moving in and out of your body. Choose a mantra that resonates with you, and repeat it silently in your mind. If your mind wanders, gently bring it back to the mantra.

Yoga Meditation:

Yoga meditation is a practice that combines physical postures, breathing techniques, and meditation. It is a holistic approach to wellness that can help you to reduce stress and anxiety, improve your flexibility and strength, and connect with your inner self.

To practice yoga meditation, find a quiet and comfortable place to practice yoga. Choose a series of postures that resonate with you, and practice them slowly and mindfully. As you move through the postures, focus on your breath and the sensations in your body. After the postures, sit in meditation for a few minutes, focusing on your breath and any thoughts, feelings, or sensations that arise.

Guided Meditation:

Guided meditation is a type of meditation that involves listening to a guided audio recording or a live instructor. It is a great option for beginners or anyone who needs a little extra support in their meditation practice. Guided meditation can help you to reduce stress and anxiety, improve your focus and concentration, and connect with your inner self.

To practice guided meditation, find a quiet and comfortable place to sit or lie down. Choose a guided audio recording or attend a live meditation class. Follow the instructions of the instructor or recording, focusing on your breath and any thoughts, feelings, or sensations that arise. Allow yourself to fully immerse in the experience, and let go of any judgments or expectations.

Body Scan Meditation:

20: MEDITATION FOR TRANQUILITY: DIFFERENT TECHNIQUES TO FIND INNER PEACE

Body scan meditation is a type of meditation that involves systematically scanning your body from head to toe, and noticing any sensations or feelings that arise. It is a great technique for reducing stress and tension, and increasing body awareness.

To practice body scan meditation, find a quiet and comfortable place to sit or lie down. Close your eyes and take a few deep breaths, focusing on the sensation of air moving in and out of your body. Start at the top of your head, and slowly scan down your body, noticing any sensations or feelings that arise. Allow yourself to fully immerse in the experience, and let go of any judgments or expectations.

Chakra Meditation:

Chakra meditation is a type of meditation that involves focusing on the seven energy centers in the body, known as chakras. It is a powerful technique for balancing the energy flow in the body, and promoting physical, emotional, and spiritual healing.

To practice chakra meditation, find a quiet and comfortable place to sit or lie down. Close your eyes and take a few deep breaths, focusing on the sensation of air moving in and out of your body. Visualize each of the seven chakras, starting at the base of the spine and moving up towards the crown of the head. Focus on each chakra in turn, visualizing a bright light or energy flowing through it. Allow yourself to fully immerse in the experience, and let go of any judgments or expectations.

In conclusion, there are many different techniques of meditation that can help you find inner peace and tranquility. Each technique has its own unique benefits, and it's important to find the one that resonates with you the most. With consistent practice and dedication, meditation can help you to reduce stress and anxiety, connect with your inner self, and achieve lasting happiness.

21: Mindful Movement: The Benefits of Yoga, Tai Chi, and Other Forms of Exercise

Mindful movement, such as yoga and tai chi, has become increasingly popular over the years as a way to promote physical and mental health. These forms of exercise focus on the connection between the mind and body, helping individuals to achieve a greater sense of balance, flexibility, and inner peace. In this chapter, we'll explore the benefits of mindful movement, the different types of exercises that fall under this category, and how you can incorporate them into your daily routine.

The Benefits of Mindful Movement

There are numerous benefits to practicing mindful movement, including:

Reduced Stress and Anxiety: Mindful movement has been shown to reduce the symptoms of stress and anxiety by promoting relaxation and improving mood.

Improved Flexibility and Balance: Regular practice of mindful movement can increase flexibility and improve balance, making it easier to perform daily activities and reduce the risk of injury.

Enhanced Physical Fitness: Many forms of mindful movement, such as yoga and tai chi, are gentle on the body, making them accessible to people of all ages and fitness levels. Regular practice can improve cardiovascular health, strengthen muscles, and increase stamina.

Better Sleep: Mindful movement has been shown to improve the quality of sleep by reducing stress and promoting relaxation.

Increased Self-Awareness: Mindful movement requires individuals to pay attention to their body and breath, promoting a greater sense of self-awareness and mindfulness.

Types of Mindful Movement

There are many different types of mindful movement, including:

Yoga: Yoga is a popular form of mindful movement that originated in ancient India. It focuses on the connection between the mind, body, and breath, using various postures and breathing techniques to promote physical and mental health.

Tai Chi: Tai chi is a Chinese martial art that involves slow, flowing movements and deep breathing. It is often referred to as "moving meditation" and is believed to promote relaxation, reduce stress, and improve balance and coordination.

Pilates: Pilates is a form of exercise that focuses on strengthening the core muscles of the body. It uses a series of controlled movements and breathing techniques to improve posture, flexibility, and overall fitness.

Qigong: Qigong is a Chinese practice that combines movement, breath, and meditation to promote physical and mental health. It is often used as a form of complementary therapy for various health conditions, including chronic pain and anxiety.

Incorporating Mindful Movement into Your Daily Routine

Incorporating mindful movement into your daily routine can be a great way to promote physical and mental health. Here are some tips to help you get started:

21: MINDFUL MOVEMENT: THE BENEFITS OF YOGA, TAI CHI, AND OTHER FORMS OF EXERCISE

Start Small: If you're new to mindful movement, start with a few minutes a day and gradually increase the length of your practice.

Find a Class: Joining a class can be a great way to learn proper technique and get support from others who are also practicing mindful movement.

Make it a Habit: Set aside time each day to practice mindful movement, just like you would with any other form of exercise.

Listen to Your Body: Pay attention to your body and don't push yourself too hard. Mindful movement should be gentle and relaxing, not painful.

Have Fun: Mindful movement can be a great way to relieve stress and have fun at the same time. Try different types of exercises and find what works best for you.

Conclusion

Mindful movement is a powerful tool for promoting physical and mental health. Whether you choose yoga, tai chi, or another form of exercise, incorporating mindful movement into your daily routine can help you achieve greater balance, flexibility, and inner peace. So, take a deep breath, find a comfortable space, and start moving mindfully towards a happier, healthier you!

22: The Power of Visualization: How to Use Your Imagination to Achieve Your Goals

Introduction

Visualization is a powerful tool that can help you achieve your goals and overcome obstacles in life. It involves using your imagination to create vivid mental images of the outcomes you desire. Visualization can be used in many areas of life, including sports, business, personal development, and health.

In this chapter, we will explore the power of visualization and how to use it to achieve your goals. We will discuss the benefits of visualization, the different types of visualization, and the steps you can take to practice visualization effectively.

Benefits of Visualization

Visualization has many benefits, including:

Helps you clarify your goals: Visualization helps you define your goals and create a clear picture of what you want to achieve. This clarity makes it easier to create an action plan and work towards your goals.

Reduces stress and anxiety: Visualization can help reduce stress and anxiety by providing a mental escape from everyday worries and fears.

Boosts confidence and motivation: Visualizing success can help boost your confidence and motivation, making it easier to take action towards your goals.

Improves performance: Visualization can help you mentally rehearse for challenging situations, improving your performance when it matters most.

Types of Visualization

There are several types of visualization techniques that you can use, including:

Outcome Visualization: This involves visualizing the end result of your goal. For example, if your goal is to run a marathon, you would visualize yourself crossing the finish line.

22: THE POWER OF VISUALIZATION: HOW TO USE YOUR IMAGINATION TO ACHIEVE YOUR GOALS

Process Visualization: This involves visualizing the steps you need to take to achieve your goal. For example, if your goal is to write a book, you would visualize yourself sitting at your desk, writing each day.

Kinesthetic Visualization: This involves visualizing yourself performing a physical activity, such as a sport or dance. For example, if your goal is to learn to play basketball, you would visualize yourself dribbling, shooting, and playing defense.

Steps to Effective Visualization

To practice visualization effectively, follow these steps:

– Choose a quiet, comfortable space where you won't be interrupted.

– Get into a relaxed state by taking deep breaths or practicing meditation.

– Visualize your desired outcome or process in detail, using all your senses. Imagine what you will see, hear, feel, and even smell.

– Repeat your visualization regularly to reinforce your goal and keep it fresh in your mind.

– Take action towards your goal. Visualization is a powerful tool, but it's not enough on its own. You need to take action towards your goal to make it a reality.

Tips for Successful Visualization

Here are some additional tips to make your visualization practice more successful:

Be specific: The more specific you are in your visualization, the more effective it will be. For example, instead of visualizing yourself "exercising," visualize yourself running, lifting weights, or doing yoga.

Use positive language: Use positive language when visualizing your goal. Instead of saying "I don't want to be overweight," say "I want to be healthy and fit."

Visualize in present tense: Visualize yourself achieving your goal as if it's happening right now, in the present moment.

Engage all your senses: The more senses you engage in your

visualization, the more vivid and powerful it will be.

Make it a habit: Consistency is key. Make visualization a daily habit to keep your goals and desires at the forefront of your mind.

Conclusion

Visualization is a powerful tool that can help you achieve your goals and overcome obstacles in life. By using your imagination to create vivid mental images of the outcomes you desire, you can clarify your goals, reduce stress and anxiety, boost confidence and motivation, and improve your performance.

Remember, visualization is not a magic solution. It's a tool that can help you achieve your goals, but it requires effort and action on your part. By following the steps and tips outlined in this chapter, you can develop an effective visualization practice and start making progress towards your goals.

If you're new to visualization, it may take some time to get the hang of it. Start small and work your way up. Begin by visualizing simple goals or everyday activities, and gradually move on to more complex goals.

Also, keep in mind that visualization is just one tool in your arsenal. It's important to combine it with other self-help strategies, such as goal setting, positive affirmations, and taking action towards your goals.

In conclusion, visualization is a powerful tool that can help you achieve your goals and overcome obstacles in life. By practicing visualization regularly and using the tips outlined in this chapter, you can unlock the power of your imagination and achieve lasting happiness, inner peace, and success in all areas of your life.

23: Self-Compassion: How to Be Kind to Yourself and Others

Self-compassion is a powerful tool that can help you overcome stress and anxiety, achieve inner peace, and cultivate lasting happiness. In this chapter, we'll explore what self-compassion is, why it's important, and how you can develop it through proven self-help strategies.

What is Self-Compassion?

Self-compassion is the practice of treating yourself with kindness, understanding, and empathy, just as you would treat a close friend or loved one. It involves acknowledging your own suffering and embracing it with warmth and non-judgment, rather than harsh self-criticism or self-pity.

Self-compassion is different from self-esteem, which is often based on external factors such as achievements, appearance, or social status. Self-compassion, on the other hand, is based on the belief that all human beings are deserving of love and compassion, regardless of their accomplishments or failures.

Why is Self-Compassion Important?

23: SELF-COMPASSION: HOW TO BE KIND TO YOUR-SELF AND OTHERS

Self-compassion is important for many reasons. First, it can help you manage stress and anxiety more effectively. When you are kind and gentle with yourself, you are more likely to feel a sense of calm and inner peace, even in the face of difficult situations.

Self-compassion can also help you overcome feelings of shame and self-doubt. When you practice self-compassion, you are less likely to judge yourself harshly or compare yourself to others. Instead, you can learn to accept yourself for who you are and appreciate your strengths and weaknesses.

Additionally, self-compassion can help you cultivate more positive relationships with others. When you are kind and compassionate with yourself, you are more likely to extend that same kindness and compassion to others, which can lead to deeper and more meaningful connections.

How to Develop Self-Compassion

Developing self-compassion can take time and effort, but it is a worthwhile pursuit that can have many benefits. Here are some proven self-help strategies that can help you cultivate self-compassion:

Practice Mindfulness

Mindfulness is the practice of paying attention to the present moment with curiosity and non-judgment. When you are mindful, you can observe your thoughts and feelings without getting caught up in them, which can help you cultivate self-awareness and self-compassion.

To practice mindfulness, try setting aside a few minutes each day to simply observe your thoughts and feelings. You can do this by focusing on your breath or by simply noticing the sensations in your body. Whenever your mind wanders, gently bring your attention back to the present moment without judgment.

Challenge Your Inner Critic

Many people have an inner critic that tells them they are not good enough, smart enough, or successful enough. This inner critic can be a barrier to self-compassion, as it can create feelings of shame and self-doubt.

To challenge your inner critic, try identifying the thoughts that trigger your self-criticism. Then, ask yourself if those thoughts are really true. Are you really a failure because you made a mistake at work? Are you really unlovable because someone rejected you?

By challenging your inner critic with evidence and logic, you can learn to recognize when your self-talk is unhelpful and replace it with more compassionate and supportive thoughts.

Practice Self-Kindness

Self-kindness involves treating yourself with the same kindness and compassion that you would offer to a close friend or loved one. This can involve doing things that make you feel good, such as taking a relaxing bath or going for a walk in nature.

To practice self-kindness, try making a list of things that make you feel happy and relaxed. Then, make a commitment to do at least one of those things every day, even if you feel like you don't have time.

Cultivate Gratitude

Gratitude is the practice of focusing on the positive aspects of your life and appreciating what you have, rather than dwelling on what you lack. Cultivating gratitude can help you develop a more positive and optimistic outlook on life, which can in turn help you cultivate self-compassion.

To cultivate gratitude, try making a list of things that you are grateful for each day. This can include things like your health, your relationships, your job, or even something as simple as a beautiful sunset. By focusing on the good in your life, you can develop a sense of appreciation and contentment that can help you feel more self-compassionate.

Practice Self-Forgiveness

Self-forgiveness involves letting go of grudges and resentment towards yourself for past mistakes or shortcomings. This can be a difficult practice, but it can be incredibly liberating and can help you cultivate self-compassion.

To practice self-forgiveness, try acknowledging the mistakes or shortcomings that are causing you pain. Then, try to let go of the need to punish yourself or hold onto negative feelings. Remember that everyone makes mistakes and that forgiveness is an act of kindness towards yourself.

Seek Support

Finally, seeking support from others can be an important part of developing self-compassion. Whether it's talking to a trusted friend or family member, joining a support group, or seeing a therapist, reaching out to others can help you feel heard and understood, which can in turn help you develop greater self-compassion.

Conclusion

Self-compassion is a powerful practice that can help you overcome stress and anxiety, develop more positive relationships with others, and cultivate lasting happiness. By practicing mindfulness, challenging your inner critic, practicing self-kindness, cultivating gratitude, practicing self-forgiveness, and seeking support, you can develop greater self-compassion and live a more fulfilling and joyful life. Remember that developing self-compassion takes time and effort, but it is a journey that is well worth taking.

24: The Benefits of Creative Expression: Finding Tranquility Through Art and Music

Art and music have been used for centuries as a form of creative expression, and for good reason. The benefits of creative expression are numerous and can have a significant impact on our mental health and well-being. In this chapter, we will explore the ways in which art and music can help us achieve tranquility and overcome stress and anxiety.

Art has the power to transport us to a different world, to allow us to see things in a new light, and to help us connect with our emotions. Whether we are creating art or simply appreciating it, there are many benefits to this form of creative expression. For one, art can help us reduce stress and anxiety. When we create art, we are often so focused on the task at hand that we are able to forget about our worries and concerns. This can be incredibly therapeutic, and can help us feel more relaxed and at ease.

Another benefit of art is that it allows us to express ourselves in a way that words sometimes cannot. For those who struggle with verbal communication, art can be a powerful tool for self-expression. Through art, we can explore our emotions, work through difficult feelings, and express ourselves in a way that is both meaningful and cathartic.

Music, like art, has the power to transport us to a different world. When we listen to music, we can be transported to a different time or place, or we can simply lose ourselves in the melody and rhythm. Music has been shown to have numerous benefits for our mental health, including reducing stress and anxiety, improving mood, and even boosting cognitive function.

One of the most powerful benefits of music is its ability to evoke emotions. Certain songs can make us feel happy, sad, or nostalgic, and can even bring up memories that we thought were long forgotten. This emotional connection to music can be incredibly healing, and can help us work through difficult emotions in a way that feels safe and supportive.

In addition to its emotional benefits, music can also be a powerful tool for mindfulness and meditation. When we listen to music mindfully, we can focus on the present moment and let go of distractions and worries. This can help us achieve a sense of calm and tranquility that can be difficult to find in our busy, hectic lives.

So how can we incorporate art and music into our lives in a way that helps us achieve tranquility? One way is to make time for creative expression on a regular basis. Whether we are painting, drawing, writing, or playing an instrument, carving out time each day or week to engage in creative expression can be incredibly beneficial for our mental health and well-being.

Another way to incorporate art and music into our lives is to simply make time to appreciate them. This might mean attending a concert, visiting an art gallery, or simply listening to music while we go about our daily routines. By taking the time to appreciate art and music, we can reap the many benefits they have to offer and find moments of tranquility in our otherwise busy lives.

In conclusion, creative expression through art and music can be a powerful tool for achieving tranquility and overcoming stress and anxiety. Whether we are creating art or simply appreciating it, or listening to music mindfully, these forms of creative expression can help us connect with our emotions, work through difficult feelings, and find moments of peace and calm in our busy lives. So why not try incorporating some art and music into your life today, and see how it can help you achieve lasting happiness and inner peace?

25: Overcoming Perfectionism: How to Let Go of Unrealistic Expectations

Perfectionism can be both a blessing and a curse. On one hand, the desire to strive for excellence can motivate us to achieve our goals and pursue our passions. On the other hand, the relentless pursuit of perfection can be a source of stress, anxiety, and even depression. The problem with perfectionism is that it is often fueled by unrealistic expectations and a fear of failure. In this chapter, we will explore the root causes of perfectionism, the negative effects it can have on our lives, and practical strategies for overcoming it.

Understanding Perfectionism

Perfectionism is a personality trait characterized by a desire for flawlessness and a tendency to set unrealistically high standards for oneself. It is often accompanied by a fear of failure and a need for control. People who struggle with perfectionism may feel that they are not good enough unless they meet their own impossibly high standards.

Perfectionism can manifest in different ways. Some people are perfectionistic about their work, striving to produce flawless results at all times. Others are perfectionistic about their appearance, constantly scrutinizing themselves in the mirror and feeling inadequate if they don't meet their own standards of beauty. Still, others may be perfectionistic about their relationships, always striving to be the perfect partner or friend.

Perfectionism can be fueled by a variety of factors, including family upbringing, cultural expectations, and personal experiences. For example, a person who grew up in a household where academic achievement was highly valued may feel pressure to always perform at their best. A person who has experienced past failures or criticism may feel a need to compensate by striving for perfection.

Negative Effects of Perfectionism

While perfectionism may initially seem like a positive trait, it can have serious negative effects on our lives. Perfectionists may struggle with anxiety, stress, and depression, as they feel constant pressure to meet their own high standards. They may also experience difficulty in relationships, as their unrealistic expectations can put strain on their interactions with others. Perfectionism can also lead to procrastination and self-doubt, as the fear of failure can be paralyzing.

Overcoming Perfectionism

Overcoming perfectionism is not easy, but it is possible. Here are some strategies that can help:

Challenge Your Beliefs: Perfectionism is often fueled by irrational beliefs about the self and the world. Take some time to reflect on the beliefs that underlie your perfectionism. Ask yourself if they are truly accurate and if they serve you well. Consider adopting more realistic and compassionate beliefs, such as "I am human, and it's okay to make mistakes" or "My worth is not determined by my achievements."

Practice Self-Compassion: Perfectionists often struggle with self-criticism and harsh self-judgment. To counteract this, practice self-compassion. Treat yourself with kindness and understanding, as you would a good friend. Remind yourself that everyone makes mistakes and that it's okay to be imperfect.

25: OVERCOMING PERFECTIONISM: HOW TO LET GO OF UNREALISTIC EXPECTATIONS

Set Realistic Goals: One way to overcome perfectionism is to set more realistic goals for yourself. Instead of aiming for perfection, aim for progress. Break larger goals into smaller, more achievable steps. Celebrate your successes along the way, even if they are small.

Embrace Failure: Perfectionists often fear failure and may avoid taking risks as a result. To overcome this fear, practice embracing failure. See it as an opportunity to learn and grow, rather than a reflection of your worth. Remind yourself that even successful people experience failure along the way.

Practice Mindfulness: Mindfulness can be a powerful tool for overcoming perfectionism. By practicing mindfulness, you can learn to be more present in the moment and less focused on your own expectations and judgments. Try incorporating mindfulness practices such as meditation or yoga into your daily routine. These practices can help you develop greater awareness of your thoughts and emotions, and cultivate a sense of inner calm and acceptance.

Seek Support: Overcoming perfectionism can be challenging, and it can be helpful to seek support from others. Consider talking to a therapist or counselor who can help you work through your perfectionistic tendencies and develop more positive coping strategies. You may also find support from friends or family members who can offer encouragement and understanding.

Take Action: Finally, remember that overcoming perfectionism requires action. It's not enough to simply acknowledge your perfectionistic tendencies and wish them away. You need to actively work to change your thoughts and behaviors. This may mean practicing self-compassion when you make a mistake, setting realistic goals, or trying something new and challenging.

Conclusion

Perfectionism can be a double-edged sword, motivating us to achieve great things while also causing undue stress and anxiety. By understanding the root causes of perfectionism and developing strategies to overcome it, we can cultivate a greater sense of inner peace and happiness. Remember, it's okay to be imperfect. Embrace your flaws and celebrate your successes, no matter how small. By doing so, you can unlock the power of tranquility and live a more fulfilling life.

26: The Role of Acceptance in Achieving Tranquility

Tranquility is a state of being that many people aspire to achieve. It is a feeling of inner peace, calmness, and serenity that can be elusive in our fast-paced, stressful lives. However, achieving tranquility is not an impossible task. In fact, it is something that can be cultivated with the right mindset and strategies. In this chapter, we will explore the role of acceptance in achieving tranquility.

Acceptance is the act of acknowledging and embracing the reality of a situation, without judgment or resistance. It is a powerful tool that can help us deal with difficult emotions, circumstances, and experiences. When we accept what is happening in our lives, we can move forward with greater ease and grace, without the burden of negative emotions such as anger, frustration, or despair.

The first step in practicing acceptance is to recognize and acknowledge our thoughts and emotions. This means paying attention to the thoughts and feelings that arise in response to a situation, without judging them or trying to suppress them. We must be willing to sit with our discomfort, without trying to escape it. When we do this, we can begin

to see the situation more clearly, and gain a deeper understanding of ourselves and our reactions.

The next step is to let go of our attachment to outcomes.
This means accepting that things may not turn out the way
we want them to, and being okay with that. We must learn
to detach ourselves from our expectations, and focus instead on the present moment. When we do this, we can experience a greater sense of peace and calm, regardless of the
outcome.

Another important aspect of acceptance is self-compassion.
This means treating ourselves with kindness, understanding, and forgiveness, especially in times of difficulty. We
must learn to be gentle with ourselves, and not berate
ourselves for our perceived shortcomings or mistakes.
When we treat ourselves with compassion, we can develop a
greater sense of self-awareness and self-love, which can
help us deal with difficult situations with greater ease and
grace.

Practicing acceptance can also help us cultivate gratitude.
When we accept what is happening in our lives, we can begin to see the beauty and goodness that exists in every mo-

ment. We can learn to appreciate the small things in life, and find joy in the present moment, regardless of our circumstances. When we cultivate gratitude, we can experience greater levels of happiness, peace, and fulfillment.

In order to practice acceptance, it is important to develop a mindfulness practice. Mindfulness is the practice of being present and aware of our thoughts, feelings, and sensations, without judgment or distraction. It can help us develop a greater sense of self-awareness and inner peace, and can be a powerful tool for dealing with difficult emotions and circumstances.

In addition to mindfulness, there are many other strategies that can help us cultivate acceptance in our lives. These include meditation, journaling, talking to a trusted friend or therapist, engaging in creative activities, and practicing self-care. By incorporating these strategies into our daily lives, we can develop a greater sense of acceptance and tranquility, and live more joyful and fulfilling lives.

In conclusion, the role of acceptance in achieving tranquility cannot be overstated. Acceptance is a powerful tool that can help us deal with difficult emotions, circumstances, and experiences. By cultivating acceptance in our lives, we can experience greater levels of inner peace, calmness, and serenity, and live more joyful and fulfilling lives. So, let us embrace acceptance, and unlock the power of tranquility in our lives!

27: The Power of Laughter: The Benefits of Humor for Your Mental Health

Laughter is often referred to as the best medicine, and for good reason. The power of humor is undeniable when it comes to improving mental health and overall well-being. In this chapter, we will explore the various benefits of laughter and how you can incorporate humor into your life to unlock the power of tranquility.

First and foremost, laughter is a natural stress-reliever. When you laugh, your body releases endorphins, which are feel-good chemicals that help to reduce stress and anxiety. This is why you may feel a sense of relief or relaxation after a good laugh. Additionally, laughter has been shown to lower cortisol levels, which is a hormone associated with stress.

Laughter also has physical benefits. It can boost your immune system, lower blood pressure, and even improve your heart health. Studies have shown that laughing can increase blood flow and oxygenation, which can help to improve cardiovascular health. Additionally, laughter has been linked to pain relief and improved muscle function.

But the benefits of laughter go beyond just physical health. It can also have a significant impact on your mental health. Laughing can help to improve your mood, reduce feelings of depression, and increase feelings of happiness and contentment. This is because laughter triggers the release of dopamine, a neurotransmitter associated with pleasure and reward.

In fact, laughter has been used as a form of therapy for many years. Laughter therapy, also known as humor therapy, involves using humor and laughter to promote healing and improve overall well-being. This type of therapy has been used to help people with a range of conditions, including depression, anxiety, chronic pain, and cancer.

So how can you incorporate more laughter into your life? Here are a few tips:

Watch a comedy. Whether it's a stand-up special or a sitcom, watching something funny can help to boost your mood and make you laugh.

27: THE POWER OF LAUGHTER: THE BENEFITS OF HUMOR FOR YOUR MENTAL HEALTH

Spend time with funny people. Surrounding yourself with people who make you laugh can help to improve your overall well-being. Schedule a night with your funniest friends or spend time with a coworker who always makes you chuckle.

Read a funny book. There are plenty of humorous books out there that can make you laugh out loud. Pick up a copy of a comedic memoir or a satirical novel and see how it affects your mood.

Practice self-deprecating humor. Laughing at yourself can be a great way to take the pressure off and find humor in even the most stressful situations.

Look for the humor in everyday situations. Sometimes, all it takes is a shift in perspective to find the humor in everyday life. Try to find the funny side of a frustrating situation or look for the humor in a mundane task.

In conclusion, laughter is a powerful tool for improving mental health and overall well-being. By incorporating humor into your life, you can reduce stress and anxiety, improve your mood, and even boost your physical health. So

go ahead and give yourself permission to laugh – your mind
and body will thank you for it.

28: Dealing with Difficult Emotions: How to Cope with Anger, Sadness, and Grief

Life is full of ups and downs, and sometimes those downs can be overwhelming. Difficult emotions like anger, sadness, and grief are part of the human experience, and everyone will face them at some point in their lives. However, it's how we cope with these emotions that determines our level of resilience and ability to bounce back from challenging situations. In this chapter, we'll explore proven self-help strategies for dealing with difficult emotions and achieving inner peace.

Anger is a powerful emotion that can manifest in a variety of ways. It can range from mild irritation to intense rage, and it can be triggered by anything from traffic congestion to a significant life event. However, when anger is not managed correctly, it can lead to destructive behaviors and harm relationships. Here are some self-help strategies for managing anger effectively:

Identify the root cause of your anger

Before you can manage your anger, you need to understand

what triggers it. Is it a certain person, situation, or circumstance? Once you identify the root cause of your anger, you can develop strategies to address it effectively.

Practice deep breathing

When you feel angry, take a few deep breaths to help you calm down. Inhale deeply through your nose, hold the breath for a few seconds, and exhale slowly through your mouth. Repeat this several times until you feel more relaxed.

Use positive self-talk

Replace negative self-talk with positive affirmations. Tell yourself that you can handle the situation and that you are in control of your emotions.

Exercise

Physical activity can help reduce tension and relieve stress. Go for a walk, run, or do some other form of exercise to help release any pent-up anger.

Seek support

28: DEALING WITH DIFFICULT EMOTIONS: HOW TO COPE WITH ANGER, SADNESS, AND GRIEF

Talking to a trusted friend or family member can help you process your anger and gain a new perspective on the situation. It's essential to seek help when you need it and not let your anger consume you.

Sadness is another challenging emotion that can be challenging to deal with. It's natural to feel sad when something doesn't go as planned, but it's crucial to ensure that sadness doesn't turn into long-term depression. Here are some self-help strategies for dealing with sadness:

Allow yourself to feel your emotions

It's okay to feel sad, and it's essential to allow yourself to feel your emotions. Acknowledge your feelings, but don't let them consume you.

Practice self-care

Self-care is crucial when you're feeling sad. Take care of your physical and emotional needs, such as getting enough sleep, eating healthy foods, and engaging in activities you enjoy.

Reach out to others

28: DEALING WITH DIFFICULT EMOTIONS: HOW TO COPE WITH ANGER, SADNESS, AND GRIEF

Don't isolate yourself when you're feeling sad. Reach out to friends and family for support. Joining a support group or talking to a therapist can also be helpful.

Engage in creative activities

Creative activities like painting, writing, or playing music can be therapeutic and help you process your emotions.

Practice gratitude

Even when you're feeling sad, it's essential to practice gratitude. Focus on the things in your life that you're thankful for and find joy in them.

Grief is a unique emotion that comes with the loss of a loved one. It's a natural process that takes time, but it's essential to find healthy ways to cope with grief to avoid long-term emotional harm. Here are some self-help strategies for dealing with grief:

Allow yourself to grieve

It's crucial to allow yourself to grieve and not suppress your emotions. Cry, scream, or express your emotions in a healthy way to help you process your grief.

Seek support

Grief can be overwhelming, and seeking support is essential. Joining a support group or talking to a therapist can help you navigate the grieving process.

Practice self-care

Taking care of yourself is essential when you're grieving. Ensure that you're getting enough sleep, eating healthy foods, and engaging in activities that bring you joy and comfort.

Honor your loved one's memory

Finding ways to honor your loved one's memory can be a healing experience. Plant a tree in their honor, create a photo album, or participate in a charity walk in their name.

Allow yourself to find joy

It's okay to find moments of joy, even when you're grieving. Laughing with friends or enjoying a beautiful sunset doesn't mean you're not honoring your loved one's memory.

In conclusion, dealing with difficult emotions can be a challenging but necessary process for achieving inner peace and lasting happiness. Whether it's anger, sadness, or grief, it's essential to find healthy ways to cope with these emotions to avoid long-term emotional harm. By identifying the root cause of your emotions, practicing self-care, seeking support, and engaging in creative activities, you can manage your emotions effectively and achieve a greater sense of tranquility in your life.

29: Overcoming Self-Doubt and Building Confidence: A Guide to Positive Self-Talk

Introduction

Self-doubt is a common feeling experienced by almost everyone at some point in their life. It can lead to a lack of confidence, low self-esteem, and even depression. Overcoming self-doubt is essential to building confidence and achieving success in life. In this chapter, we will discuss the power of positive self-talk and how it can help you overcome self-doubt and build confidence.

What is Self-Doubt?

Self-doubt is a feeling of uncertainty or lack of confidence in oneself or one's abilities. It is a negative voice in your head that tells you that you are not good enough, smart enough, or capable enough. Self-doubt can be triggered by a variety of factors such as failure, rejection, criticism, or fear of the unknown.

Why is Self-Doubt Harmful?

29: OVERCOMING SELF-DOUBT AND BUILDING CON-FIDENCE: A GUIDE TO POSITIVE SELF-TALK

Self-doubt can be harmful as it can prevent you from reaching your full potential. It can hold you back from taking risks, pursuing your dreams, and achieving your goals. Self-doubt can also lead to negative thoughts and feelings such as anxiety, depression, and low self-esteem. It is important to learn how to overcome self-doubt to avoid these negative consequences.

What is Positive Self-Talk?

Positive self-talk is a technique used to combat negative thoughts and feelings. It involves replacing negative self-talk with positive affirmations and messages. Positive self-talk can help you build confidence, reduce stress, and improve your overall well-being.

Steps to Overcoming Self-Doubt and Building Confidence

Step 1: Identify Negative Self-Talk

The first step in overcoming self-doubt is to identify negative self-talk. Pay attention to the negative messages you tell yourself and the situations that trigger them. Write them down so you can recognize them and replace them with positive self-talk.

Step 2: Challenge Negative Self-Talk

Once you have identified negative self-talk, challenge it. Ask yourself if it is true and provide evidence to support or refute it. If it is not true, replace it with a positive message. For example, if you tell yourself that you are not good enough, challenge this thought by listing your accomplishments and strengths.

Step 3: Practice Positive Self-Talk

Practice positive self-talk daily. Create a list of positive affirmations and messages and repeat them to yourself regularly. Some examples include "I am capable and competent," "I am worthy of love and respect," and "I am confident in myself and my abilities."

Step 4: Surround Yourself with Positive People

Surround yourself with positive people who support and encourage you. Avoid negative people who bring you down and trigger self-doubt.

29: OVERCOMING SELF-DOUBT AND BUILDING CONFIDENCE: A GUIDE TO POSITIVE SELF-TALK

Step 5: Take Action

Take action to overcome self-doubt. Face your fears and take risks. Start small and work your way up. Celebrate your successes and learn from your failures.

Conclusion

Overcoming self-doubt is essential to building confidence and achieving success in life. Positive self-talk is a powerful tool that can help you overcome self-doubt and build confidence. By following the steps outlined in this chapter, you can learn to replace negative self-talk with positive affirmations and messages, surround yourself with positive people, and take action to achieve your goals. Remember, you are capable and competent, and you deserve to achieve your dreams.

30: Developing a Mindful Work Life: Finding Tranquility in Your Career

In today's fast-paced world, the pressure to succeed in our careers can cause stress and anxiety. We often find ourselves chasing promotions, working longer hours, and sacrificing our personal lives to advance our professional goals. However, this approach can be counterproductive and may eventually lead to burnout. In this chapter, we'll explore how to develop a mindful work-life and find tranquility in our careers.

Define Your Purpose

The first step towards developing a mindful work-life is to define your purpose. Ask yourself, what is it that you want to achieve in your career? Is it financial stability, personal fulfillment, or making a difference in the world? Defining your purpose will help you stay focused and motivated in your career.

Set Realistic Goals

Once you have defined your purpose, it's time to set realistic goals. Break down your purpose into smaller, achievable goals. For instance, if your purpose is financial stability, set a goal to save a certain amount of money each month. If your purpose is personal fulfillment, set a goal to learn a new skill or take on a challenging project at work.

Practice Mindfulness

Mindfulness is the practice of being fully present and engaged in the moment. When we practice mindfulness, we can reduce stress and anxiety and increase our focus and productivity. To practice mindfulness at work, try the following:

– Take a few deep breaths before starting your workday.

– Set aside time each day to meditate or practice deep breathing exercises.

– Take breaks throughout the day to stretch and clear your mind.

– Focus on one task at a time and avoid multitasking.

Prioritize Self-Care

30: DEVELOPING A MINDFUL WORK LIFE: FINDING TRANQUILITY IN YOUR CAREER

Self-care is essential for maintaining a healthy work-life balance. It's important to prioritize self-care to prevent burnout and improve overall well-being. Here are some ways to prioritize self-care:

– Get enough sleep each night.

– Exercise regularly.

– Eat a balanced diet.

– Take breaks throughout the day to recharge.

– Engage in activities that bring you joy and relaxation.

Cultivate Positive Relationships

Positive relationships are crucial for a healthy work-life balance. Cultivate positive relationships with your coworkers, managers, and clients. Here are some tips for cultivating positive relationships:

– Communicate effectively and respectfully.

– Listen actively to others.

30: DEVELOPING A MINDFUL WORK LIFE: FINDING TRANQUILITY IN YOUR CAREER

– Collaborate with others to achieve common goals.

– Express gratitude and appreciation for others' contributions.

Manage Time Effectively

Effective time management is essential for a productive and stress-free work-life. Here are some tips for managing time effectively:

– Prioritize tasks based on their importance and urgency.

– Create a to-do list each day and update it regularly.

– Break down large tasks into smaller, more manageable tasks.

– Use a calendar or scheduling tool to keep track of appointments and deadlines.

Seek Support

Finally, don't be afraid to seek support when you need it. Whether it's talking to a trusted friend or colleague, seeking professional counseling, or joining a support group, there are many resources available to help you manage stress and anxiety in your career.

In conclusion, developing a mindful work-life is essential for finding tranquility in your career. By defining your purpose, setting realistic goals, practicing mindfulness, prioritizing self-care, cultivating positive relationships, managing time effectively, and seeking support when needed, you can achieve lasting happiness and success in your career.

31: The Importance of Boundaries: How to Establish Healthy Limits in Your Life

In today's fast-paced world, where we are constantly bombarded with information, demands, and responsibilities, it's easy to feel overwhelmed and stressed out. We often find ourselves juggling multiple tasks and responsibilities, and we rarely take time for ourselves to relax and recharge. This can lead to feelings of burnout, exhaustion, and even anxiety.

The key to overcoming these feelings and achieving lasting happiness is to establish healthy boundaries in your life. Boundaries are limits that you set for yourself to protect your physical, emotional, and mental well-being. They help you establish a sense of control and balance in your life, and they allow you to prioritize what is truly important.

In this chapter, we will discuss the importance of boundaries and how to establish healthy limits in your life. We will explore the benefits of setting boundaries, the different types of boundaries, and practical strategies for implementing them.

31: THE IMPORTANCE OF BOUNDARIES: HOW TO ESTABLISH HEALTHY LIMITS IN YOUR LIFE

The Benefits of Setting Boundaries

Setting boundaries is essential for achieving inner peace and happiness. Here are some of the key benefits of establishing healthy limits in your life:

Reduced stress and anxiety: When you set boundaries, you create a sense of control over your life, which can help reduce stress and anxiety.

Increased self-esteem: When you set boundaries and stick to them, you send a message to yourself and others that you value yourself and your well-being. This can increase your self-esteem and confidence.

Improved relationships: Boundaries help you establish clear expectations and communicate your needs effectively, which can improve your relationships with others.

Increased productivity: When you set boundaries, you prioritize what is truly important, which can help you focus on your goals and achieve more in less time.

Types of Boundaries

31: THE IMPORTANCE OF BOUNDARIES: HOW TO ESTABLISH HEALTHY LIMITS IN YOUR LIFE

There are several different types of boundaries that you can establish in your life. Here are some of the most common:

Physical boundaries: These boundaries involve your personal space and physical needs. For example, you might set a physical boundary by not allowing others to touch you without your consent.

Emotional boundaries: These boundaries involve your emotional needs and feelings. For example, you might set an emotional boundary by not allowing others to criticize or belittle you.

Time boundaries: These boundaries involve your time and how you spend it. For example, you might set a time boundary by not allowing others to interrupt you when you are working or spending time with family.

Social boundaries: These boundaries involve your social interactions and relationships. For example, you might set a social boundary by not allowing toxic people into your life.

Establishing Healthy Boundaries

Now that we have discussed the importance of boundaries

and the different types of boundaries, let's explore some practical strategies for establishing healthy limits in your life:

Identify your needs: The first step in establishing healthy boundaries is to identify your needs. Take some time to reflect on what is truly important to you and what you need to feel happy and fulfilled.

Communicate your boundaries: Once you have identified your needs, it's important to communicate your boundaries to others. Be clear and assertive when communicating your boundaries, and don't be afraid to say no when necessary.

Practice self-care: Self-care is essential for maintaining healthy boundaries. Make time for yourself to do things that you enjoy, and prioritize activities that help you relax and recharge.

Set realistic expectations: Setting realistic expectations for yourself and others is key to establishing healthy boundaries. Don't take on more than you can handle, and be realistic about what you can accomplish in a given day.

Be consistent: Finally, it's important to be consistent in enforcing your boundaries. Stick to your boundaries even when it's difficult, and don't allow others to push you past your limits.

Conclusion

Establishing healthy boundaries is essential for achieving inner peace, overcoming stress and anxiety, and achieving lasting happiness. By setting limits on what you are willing to tolerate, you create a sense of control and balance in your life. This allows you to prioritize what is truly important and focus on your goals.

It's important to remember that boundaries are not about being selfish or pushing others away. Instead, they are about protecting your physical, emotional, and mental well-being. When you establish healthy boundaries, you create a positive cycle of self-care and self-respect that can improve all areas of your life.

In conclusion, setting boundaries is an essential part of achieving tranquility and lasting happiness. By identifying your needs, communicating your boundaries, practicing self-care, setting realistic expectations, and being consistent, you can establish healthy limits in your life and unlock the power of tranquility. Remember that boundaries are not about limiting yourself, but about creating a healthy and fulfilling life that allows you to thrive.

32: Finding Tranquility in Solitude: The Benefits of Alone Time

Solitude, the state of being alone, is often viewed as a negative thing in our society. People are social beings and are expected to interact with others to maintain a healthy mental state. However, what if I told you that solitude can actually be a powerful tool in finding inner peace, overcoming stress and anxiety, and achieving lasting happiness? In this chapter, we will explore the benefits of alone time and how to make the most out of it.

The Benefits of Solitude

When we are alone, we are free to explore our inner selves without any external distractions. This introspection can help us gain a deeper understanding of our thoughts, feelings, and behaviors. In turn, this understanding can lead to self-improvement and personal growth. Moreover, being alone can provide us with the opportunity to recharge our batteries and renew our energy. When we are constantly surrounded by people, we are bombarded with their thoughts, emotions, and problems, which can be emotionally draining. Spending time alone can give us the chance to disconnect from these negative influences and focus on our own well-being.

Additionally, being alone can foster creativity and innovation. When we are not constantly exposed to the ideas and opinions of others, we are free to think outside the box and come up with novel solutions to problems. This is because solitude can give us the mental space we need to generate new ideas and perspectives.

Lastly, solitude can help us build resilience and emotional intelligence. When we are alone, we are forced to confront our fears, anxieties, and negative thoughts. This can be challenging at first, but with practice, we can learn to overcome these obstacles and build our emotional strength. Moreover, being alone can help us develop empathy and compassion for ourselves and others. When we are more in touch with our own emotions and thoughts, we are better equipped to understand the feelings of others.

Making the Most of Alone Time

Now that we know the benefits of alone time, how can we

make the most of it? Here are some tips to help you maximize your alone time:

Plan ahead: Set aside specific times during the week for alone time. This can be as simple as waking up 30 minutes earlier in the morning or dedicating an hour in the evening to yourself.

Disconnect: Turn off your phone, computer, and any other electronic devices that can be a source of distraction. This will help you focus on the present moment and eliminate any external stimuli.

Engage in mindfulness practices: Practice meditation, deep breathing, or yoga to help you stay present and calm.

Pursue your passions: Use your alone time to pursue activities that bring you joy and fulfillment. This can be anything from reading a book to painting to going for a hike.

Journal: Write down your thoughts, feelings, and experiences during your alone time. This can help you gain insight into your inner world and identify areas for personal growth.

32: FINDING TRANQUILITY IN SOLITUDE: THE BENE-FITS OF ALONE TIME

Reflect: Use your alone time to reflect on your life goals and values. This can help you gain clarity on what you want to achieve and how you want to live your life.

Practice self-compassion: Be kind to yourself during your alone time. Acknowledge your strengths and weaknesses and celebrate your successes.

Conclusion

In conclusion, solitude can be a powerful tool in finding inner peace, overcoming stress and anxiety, and achieving lasting happiness. By taking the time to disconnect from external distractions and focus on our inner selves, we can gain a deeper understanding of our thoughts, feelings, and behaviors. Additionally, being alone can foster creativity, build resilience, and help us develop empathy and compassion. So, don't be afraid to carve out some alone time for yourself. Embrace the quiet moments and use them to nurture your inner world.

33: Mindful Parenting: How to Raise Children in a Tranquil Environment

Parenting is one of the most rewarding yet challenging roles in life. It comes with a lot of responsibilities and can be overwhelming at times. However, when you embrace mindfulness, you can raise children in a tranquil environment that promotes their emotional, physical, and mental well-being. In this chapter, we will explore how to cultivate mindful parenting and create a peaceful atmosphere for your children to thrive.

What is Mindful Parenting?

Mindful parenting is the practice of being present and fully engaged in the parenting experience. It involves being aware of your emotions, thoughts, and behaviors, and how they impact your child. Mindful parenting helps you to respond to your child's needs with love, kindness, and compassion, rather than reacting impulsively to their behavior. It also helps you to create a nurturing and secure environment that promotes your child's emotional, physical, and mental health.

33: MINDFUL PARENTING: HOW TO RAISE CHILDREN IN A TRANQUIL ENVIRONMENT

Benefits of Mindful Parenting

Practicing mindful parenting has numerous benefits for both you and your child. Here are some of the benefits:

Reduced stress and anxiety: Mindful parenting can help you reduce stress and anxiety by increasing your awareness of your emotions and thoughts. When you are more aware of your internal experiences, you are less likely to get overwhelmed by them.

Improved communication: Mindful parenting can improve communication between you and your child. When you are fully present, you can better understand your child's needs and respond in a way that meets those needs.

Increased emotional regulation: Mindful parenting can help you regulate your emotions better, which can positively impact your child's emotional regulation. When you are calm and composed, your child is more likely to feel safe and secure.

Better parent-child relationship: Mindful parenting can help you build a better relationship with your child. When you are present, attentive, and compassionate, your child feels heard and understood.

Improved child development: Mindful parenting can promote your child's emotional, physical, and mental development. When your child feels safe, secure, and loved, they are more likely to thrive.

How to Cultivate Mindful Parenting

Practice self-care: Taking care of yourself is essential to being a mindful parent. Make time for self-care activities such as meditation, exercise, or reading a book. When you are calm and centered, you are better equipped to handle the challenges of parenting.

Be present: Being fully present is key to practicing mindful parenting. When you are with your child, put away distractions such as your phone and focus on them. Listen to what they are saying and respond in a way that shows you are fully engaged.

Practice active listening: Active listening involves giving your full attention to your child when they are speaking. It means not interrupting them, not judging them, and responding with empathy and understanding.

Show empathy: Empathy is the ability to understand and share the feelings of another person. When you show empathy to your child, you validate their emotions and help them feel heard and understood.

Practice positive discipline: Positive discipline involves setting clear boundaries and consequences for your child's behavior, while also promoting their emotional and social development. It involves using positive reinforcement, such as praise and rewards, rather than punishment.

Practice gratitude: Practicing gratitude involves focusing on the positive aspects of your life and expressing gratitude for them. When you practice gratitude, you model positive thinking for your child and help them develop a positive outlook on life.

Foster a positive home environment: Creating a positive home environment involves setting a positive tone, establishing routines and rituals, and promoting a sense of belonging and security for your child. This can include things like family dinners, game nights, or other fun activities that promote family bonding.

Conclusion

Mindful parenting involves being present, attentive, and compassionate to your child's needs. It requires practice, patience, and a willingness to learn and grow as a parent. By embracing mindful parenting, you can create a peaceful and nurturing environment for your child to thrive.

Remember that parenting is a journey, and it is okay to make mistakes along the way. Be gentle with yourself and your child, and approach each day with a sense of curiosity and openness. With the right mindset and tools, you can raise children who are emotionally, physically, and mentally healthy, and who have the skills they need to navigate the challenges of life with confidence and resilience.

In summary, mindful parenting is a powerful tool for promoting tranquility in your family. By cultivating awareness, empathy, and positive discipline, you can create a home environment that supports your child's growth and development, while also promoting your own emotional wellbeing.

33: MINDFUL PARENTING: HOW TO RAISE CHILDREN IN A TRANQUIL ENVIRONMENT

With these strategies in mind, you can unlock the power of tranquility and enjoy a more peaceful, fulfilling life as a parent.

34: The Role of Spirituality in Achieving Tranquility

In today's fast-paced world, achieving tranquility can feel like an impossible task. Our busy lives are filled with stress, anxiety, and constant stimulation, leaving little time for relaxation and self-reflection. However, there is a powerful tool that can help us achieve inner peace and overcome the challenges of modern life: spirituality.

Spirituality can mean different things to different people. For some, it may involve religious practices, such as prayer or attending services. For others, it may be a more personal journey of self-discovery, involving meditation, mindfulness, or other spiritual practices. Whatever form it takes, spirituality can provide a sense of purpose, connection, and inner strength that can help us navigate life's ups and downs with greater ease and resilience.

One of the key benefits of spirituality is that it can help us develop a sense of inner calm and tranquility. By connecting with something greater than ourselves – whether that be a higher power, the natural world, or our own inner wisdom – we can find a sense of peace and perspective that can help us overcome the stresses and anxieties of daily life. This can be especially valuable in times of crisis or uncertainty, when we may feel overwhelmed or lost.

Another way that spirituality can help us achieve tranquility is by fostering a sense of gratitude and appreciation for the present moment. When we are focused on the past or the future, we may feel anxious or stressed about things we can't control. However, by cultivating mindfulness and staying present in the moment, we can learn to appreciate the beauty and abundance of life as it is right now. This can help us feel more grounded, centered, and at peace, even in the midst of challenging circumstances.

Spirituality can also provide a sense of purpose and meaning that can help us feel more fulfilled and content. When we have a strong sense of connection to something greater than ourselves, we may feel more motivated to live our lives with intention and purpose, striving to make a positive impact in the world around us. This can help us feel a sense of fulfillment and satisfaction that can contribute to our overall sense of happiness and well-being.

Of course, developing a spiritual practice is not always easy. It can require time, effort, and commitment, and may involve confronting difficult emotions or beliefs. However, the rewards of a spiritual practice can be profound, offering us a sense of peace, purpose, and resilience that can help us thrive in the face of life's challenges.

If you are interested in exploring spirituality as a path to tranquility, there are many different approaches you can try. Here are a few ideas to get you started:

Meditation: This is one of the most common spiritual practices, and for good reason. Regular meditation can help you develop greater mindfulness, awareness, and inner calm. There are many different types of meditation, so experiment to find the approach that works best for you.

Prayer: If you are religious, prayer can be a powerful way to connect with a higher power and find a sense of peace and guidance. Even if you are not religious, you can still try prayer as a way to express gratitude or connect with something greater than yourself.

Nature walks: Spending time in nature can be a powerful spiritual practice, helping you connect with the natural world and find a sense of peace and tranquility. Try going for a walk in the woods, sitting by a river, or simply spending time in your backyard or local park.

Journaling: Writing can be a powerful tool for self-reflection and personal growth. Try keeping a journal to explore your thoughts, emotions, and beliefs, and to track your progress as you explore your spiritual path.

Yoga: This ancient practice can help you develop greater flexibility, strength, and inner peace. Yoga involves a series of poses and breathing exercises that can help you connect with your body and cultivate a sense of mindfulness and inner calm.

Gratitude practice: Cultivating a sense of gratitude can be a powerful spiritual practice that can help you focus on the present moment and appreciate the abundance in your life. Try writing down three things you are grateful for each day, or taking a few moments each morning to reflect on what you appreciate in your life.

Mindful eating: Eating mindfully can be a powerful spiritual practice that can help you connect with your body and appreciate the nourishment and sustenance that food provides. Try slowing down and savoring each bite, paying attention to the textures, flavors, and aromas of your food.

Volunteering: Giving back to others can be a powerful way to connect with a sense of purpose and meaning. Try volunteering for a cause that is meaningful to you, and notice how it makes you feel to make a positive impact in the world around you.

Whatever approach you choose, it is important to remember that spirituality is a personal journey, and there is no one-size-fits-all approach. Take the time to explore different practices, and notice what feels most meaningful and nourishing to you.

As you explore your spiritual path, it is also important to remember that it is not a quick fix or a one-time solution. Rather, it is a lifelong journey of growth, self-discovery, and personal evolution. Be patient with yourself, and approach your spiritual practice with a sense of curiosity and openness.

In conclusion, spirituality can be a powerful tool for achieving tranquility, inner peace, and lasting happiness. By connecting with something greater than ourselves, cultivating mindfulness and gratitude, and finding a sense of purpose and meaning, we can navigate life's challenges with greater ease and resilience. If you are interested in exploring spirituality as a path to tranquility, there are many different approaches you can try. The key is to find the practices that resonate most deeply with you, and to approach your spiritual journey with an open mind and heart.

35: The Benefits of Community: Building Connections for a More Tranquil Life

In our fast-paced world, it can be easy to feel disconnected from others. We spend our days rushing from one obligation to the next, and often forget to take the time to connect with the people around us. However, the benefits of building a sense of community cannot be overstated. In this chapter, we will explore how connecting with others can help us achieve a more tranquil life.

First and foremost, building a sense of community can help us feel less alone. When we are going through a difficult time, it can be easy to feel like we are the only ones struggling. However, when we connect with others and share our experiences, we realize that we are not alone. This can help us feel more supported, and can even help us find solutions to our problems.

Additionally, building a sense of community can help us feel more purposeful. When we connect with others and work together towards a common goal, we feel like we are a part of something bigger than ourselves. This can be incredibly fulfilling and can give us a sense of purpose that we may not have otherwise.

Building a sense of community can also help us develop more meaningful relationships. When we take the time to connect with others, we are able to develop deeper, more meaningful relationships. These relationships can provide us with emotional support, and can even help us navigate difficult times in our lives.

Furthermore, building a sense of community can help us develop empathy and compassion for others. When we connect with others and learn about their experiences, we are able to develop a better understanding of their perspectives. This can help us become more empathetic and compassionate, and can even help us become better problem-solvers.

Finally, building a sense of community can help us achieve a more tranquil life by providing us with a support system. When we have a community of people who care about us and support us, we are better equipped to handle stress and difficult situations. This can help us achieve a sense of inner peace and tranquility that we may not have otherwise.

35: THE BENEFITS OF COMMUNITY: BUILDING CONNECTIONS FOR A MORE TRANQUIL LIFE

So, how can we build a sense of community in our lives? There are many different strategies that we can use, depending on our individual preferences and circumstances. Some people may find it helpful to join a club or organization that aligns with their interests. Others may prefer to volunteer or participate in community events. Still others may find it helpful to connect with others online or through social media.

Regardless of the specific strategies we use, the key is to take the time to connect with others and build meaningful relationships. By doing so, we can reap the many benefits of community and achieve a more tranquil life.

36: Living a Tranquil Life: Bringing Inner Peace and Happiness to Your Everyday Experience

In today's world, with its fast-paced, ever-changing nature, it can be difficult to find a sense of inner peace and tranquility. From the stresses of work and finances to the challenges of personal relationships, it's easy to feel overwhelmed and anxious. But what if there was a way to bring more calm and tranquility to your everyday experience?

The good news is that it is possible to live a tranquil life, even in the midst of chaos and uncertainty. By learning to cultivate inner peace and harness the power of self-help strategies, you can achieve lasting happiness and overcome stress and anxiety.

In this chapter, we'll explore some proven techniques for living a tranquil life. From mindfulness and meditation to gratitude and self-care, these strategies can help you find greater calm and serenity in your daily life.

The Power of Mindfulness

Mindfulness is the practice of being fully present and engaged in the current moment, without judgment or distraction. When we practice mindfulness, we become more aware of our thoughts, emotions, and physical sensations, and we learn to observe them without getting caught up in them.

One of the benefits of mindfulness is that it can help us manage stress and anxiety. When we're mindful, we're less likely to get lost in worries about the future or regrets about the past. Instead, we focus on the here and now, which can help us feel more grounded and centered.

There are many ways to practice mindfulness, from sitting meditation to mindful walking or eating. One simple technique is to take a few deep breaths and focus your attention on the sensations of your breath as it enters and leaves your body. Whenever your mind wanders, gently bring your focus back to your breath.

Another technique is to practice mindful listening. The next time you're having a conversation with someone, try to really listen to what they're saying without interrupting or getting distracted. Focus on their words, tone of voice, and body language, and try to be fully present in the conversation.

Mindful movement practices, such as yoga or tai chi, can also be a great way to cultivate mindfulness while also improving physical health and flexibility.

By incorporating mindfulness into your daily routine, you can develop a greater sense of inner peace and tranquility.

The Benefits of Meditation

Meditation is another powerful tool for cultivating inner peace and tranquility. Like mindfulness, meditation involves focusing your attention and training your mind to stay in the present moment.

There are many different types of meditation, from guided meditations to silent meditation. One common technique is to sit quietly with your eyes closed, and focus your attention on your breath. Whenever your mind wanders, simply bring your attention back to your breath.

Meditation has been shown to have numerous benefits, including reducing stress and anxiety, improving focus and concentration, and promoting feelings of calm and relaxation. Regular meditation practice can also help you develop greater self-awareness and insight into your thoughts and emotions.

If you're new to meditation, it can be helpful to start with shorter sessions, such as five or ten minutes a day, and gradually work your way up to longer sessions. You can also try using guided meditation apps or videos to help you get started.

Gratitude and Positivity

Focusing on gratitude and positivity can also be a powerful way to cultivate inner peace and tranquility. When we focus on what we're thankful for and look for the good in our lives, we shift our perspective and create a more positive mindset.

One way to cultivate gratitude is to keep a gratitude journal, where you write down things you're thankful for each day. This can be as simple as a good cup of coffee or a phone call from a friend. By focusing on the positives in our lives, we can start to feel more content and fulfilled.

Another technique is to practice positive affirmations, where you repeat positive statements to yourself, such as "I am strong and capable" or "I am deserving of love and happiness." By focusing on positive self-talk, we can build self-confidence and cultivate a more positive outlook on life.

Self-Care and Boundaries

Finally, taking care of ourselves and setting healthy boundaries can also be important for living a tranquil life. When we prioritize our own needs and make time for self-care, we're better equipped to handle stress and challenges in our daily lives.

Self-care can look different for everyone, but some common practices include getting enough sleep, eating well, and making time for activities you enjoy. It's also important to set healthy boundaries with others, whether that means saying no to requests that don't align with your values or taking a break from social media when it feels overwhelming.

36: LIVING A TRANQUIL LIFE: BRINGING INNER PEACE AND HAPPINESS TO YOUR EVERYDAY EXPERIENCE

By prioritizing our own needs and setting healthy boundaries, we can create a greater sense of inner peace and tranquility in our daily lives.

Conclusion

Living a tranquil life is not about avoiding stress or challenges altogether. Rather, it's about learning to cultivate inner peace and harnessing the power of self-help strategies to manage stress and anxiety in healthy ways.

By practicing mindfulness and meditation, focusing on gratitude and positivity, and prioritizing self-care and healthy boundaries, you can achieve lasting happiness and overcome the challenges of daily life with greater ease and resilience.

Thank You

As we reach the end of this book, I want to say thanks for reading this book.

I want to get this information out to as many people as possible. If you found this book helpful, I would greatly appreciate you leaving me a review. This helps others find the book as well.

Disclaimer

This document is geared towards providing exact and reliable information in regards to the topic and issue covered. The publication is sold on the idea that the publisher is not required to render an accounting, officially permitted, or otherwise, qualified services. If advice is necessary, legal, financial, medical or professional, a practiced individual in the profession should be ordered.

This information is not presented by a financial or medical practitioner and is for entertainment, educational and informational purposes only. The content is not intended as a substitute for professional medical advice, diagnosis, or treatment. Always seek the advice of your physician or other qualified health care provider with any questions you may have regarding a medical condition. Never disregard professional medical advice or delay in seeking it because of something you have read.

The information provided herein is stated to be truthful and consistent, in that any liability, in terms of inattention or otherwise, by any usage or abuse of any policies, processes, or directions contained within is the solitary and utter responsibility of the recipient reader. Under no circumstances

DISCLAIMER

will any legal responsibility or blame be held against the publisher for any reparation, damages, or monetary loss due to the information herein, either directly or indirectly.